WALKING
WITH
YESHUA

WALKING WITH YESHUA

Beginning Steps For New Believers

DEREK LEMAN

Messianic Jewish Publishers
a division of
Messianic Jewish Communications
Baltimore, Maryland

Unless otherwise noted, all Scripture quotations are taken from the *Complete Jewish Bible*. Copyright by David H. Stern, Jewish New Testament Publications, Inc., 2000.

Also quoted is the NASB.

© 2000 by Derek Leman
All rights reserved. Published 2000.
Printed in the United States of America.
Cover design by Drawing Board Studios

05 04 03 02 01 00   6 5 4 3 2 1

ISBN 1-880226-89-8

Library of Congress classification number 00-133469

Lederer/Messianic Jewish Publishers
a division of
Messianic Jewish Communications
6204 Park Heights Avenue
Baltimore, Maryland 21215
(410) 358-6471

Distributed by
Messianic Jewish Resources International
Individual order line: (800) 410-7367
Trade order line: (800) 773-MJRI (6574)
E-mail: lederer@messianicjewish.net
Website: www.messianicjewish.net

CONTENTS

INTRODUCTION

How To Use This Book

An anonymous writer once described life as a torturous path through a forest. We are all walking backwards and cannot see what lies before us. Others are further down the path than we are and can warn us of pitfalls and hazards. Although it may be hard to imagine now, the life of faith is not just a day at the park. There are hazards to avoid. Starting out on the road of faith with Yeshua requires some input and insight from those who have been walking with him for a while. This book is a tool to help you, but more than a book is needed. It is vital that you surround yourself with other believers, who are further down the road.

Making this journey with Yeshua without the help of your fellow travelers is not a great idea. Neither is blindly following everything that others tell you. As you go, you will learn how to tell for yourself what God teaches and how God wants us to live. For now you have to be somewhat trusting of other believers, especially of spiritual leaders at the congregation you are attending.

Probably the wisest and most important thing you can do for yourself right now is to find someone at your congregation who is a wise believer. This person ought to be the same gender as yourself if possible. Your congregational leaders should be able to help you find someone (or they may have already) who can go through the material in this book with you. They will be able to add to the content of the book.

Books can communicate ideas, but they cannot communicate the warmth of emotion that a worshipful moment brings. Nor can written words describe accurately the experience of God. Knowing God is more than knowing about him. It is experiencing him. If you read this book and go through the study guides on your own, you will learn a great deal. But you will miss a major part of the picture. Go on ahead and read through this section and begin reading the next section, "Getting Started." Have someone able to go with you through the rest of the book adding his or her insights and experiences. In the lingo of the Bible, you will be discipled by this person. Discipling literally means teaching, but with the connotation of direct, personal, face-to-face involvement from the discipler and commitment and submission from the disciple.

You will not only need other believers to help you know God, but you will need the teachings of the Bible. The fact is that some things that are wrong can seem right, if people call them "Messianic Jewish" or "Christian." There are many groups who call themselves "Messianic Jewish" or "Christian" who do not believe what the Bible teaches. They will always quote from the Bible, which can be confusing, but they interpret it incorrectly. Remember that the devil himself quotes Scripture, as he did to Yeshua in the temptation (Matt. 4:1–11).

While all of this can make you afraid of the future, don't be afraid. Just learn from the Bible (this book is a beginning to that process), and from your spiritual leaders and other believers. It won't be long before you'll know enough to help others. You'll probably find yourself telling others about God. Disciples tend to make other disciples; that is the way of things. For now, just rejoice in the fact that you have come into an inheritance from God that can never fade. Through Yeshua, you have become a child of the king.

What Lies Ahead of You in This Book

Following this chapter, you will begin your journey with "Getting Started." This section will prepare you to give beginning answers to some of the questions that may come your way. It will help you to know how to deal with family, to understand that God accepts you in Yeshua, to know about the new life you have come to in Yeshua, and to understand the immersion ceremony.

Next, you will find a study section called "Beginning Steps." Each chapter of beginning steps is intended to be a weekly lesson with the involvement of a discipler. You should do the work before the discipler meets with you and discuss your answers with him or her. Then do the daily homework for the rest of the week.

The next section is similar: "Deeper Issues." Do these lessons and discuss them with your discipler. Each day work on the homework. When you have finished these sections, you have graduated from Faith 101. You are a bona fide kindergartner in the faith. But there is more to read to prepare you for elementary school.

The last two sections are for you to read. You should also discuss them with your discipler, though things could be more relaxed and less formal at this point. "Potential Problem Areas" is rather deep. There are certain issues that can be a source of argument. The issues covered are especially important for Jewish and non-Jewish believers in Messianic Jewish congregations. There may be a viewpoint or two expressed in this book that your own congregational leaders disagree with. The main thing is to avoid allowing these issues to turn into a source of argument. Over time you will learn a great deal more about these issues than this book can cover. These chapters are just an introduction.

"A Messianic Jewish Lifestyle" is a section finally for you to learn the basics of Jewish customs as well as biblical commandments. Much of what you will see among Jewish believers is merely tradition. You will need to learn to separate the "I-must-do-these things" from the "I-enjoy-doing-these things."

May God bless you as you set out on his road. He has already promised that you will make it to the end if you believe. He hasn't promised that you will make it without pitfalls and rabbit trails. But with faith, obedience, and love you will not only make it to the end, you will finish the race a winner. You will be gathered into Yeshua's arms and hear the sweetest words anyone could ever hear from him: "Well done, good and faithful servant."

A Note For Disciplers

The basic intellectual material needed by new believers is already in this book. It is the heart material and the practical experience that you must add. Don't think of your job as simply a grader. You are to be a living example of these truths. Your love and warmth and joy in the faith are needed most. You have had experiences with God. Share them along the way. Open up your life to be a second book alongside this one. Share also your failings—even the embarrassing ones that people don't usually talk about (Yes, I mean even regarding sexual temptation and spiritual dryness!). Pray daily for your disciple and fulfill Yeshua's command to make disciples, immerse them, and teach them all the things he has commanded.

Section

GETTING STARTED

One

A Place of Glory

Everybody has a different story. Diane had a dreamlike vision of Yeshua (Jesus) walking in the desert near Las Vegas that started her faith journey. Sharon had been attending a Baptist church with her family for years, the only Jewish woman in that church, when she came to Yeshua in a very emotional service. Teresa found him through a series of events in her life, including a vision and a desperate time in a drug rehabilitation program. Kate came to a Messianic Jewish Bible study looking for someone to show her the way to faith in God. Nancy had a believing friend who talked to her for years, and then she suddenly realized that Yeshua is the truth and the life. I read a book, C.S. Lewis's *Mere Christianity*, starting out as a skeptic, and changed into a believer within a period of less than two hours.

Many of us resisted the truth. Friends in high school remember hearing me say that faith in God was for the weak-minded. Kate and Sharon had shown no interest for years as their husbands tried to get them to see the truth. Yet, eventually, all of us stumbled upon a new world of love, joy, and peace. We would never have thought possible the love that we now have with other believers. We couldn't imagine faith in a kingdom that is unseen and which runs on principles counter to all that we grew up believing. Love your enemies, give to those who ask of you, don't return insults, and love God more than success and enjoyment, we are now told. Who would have thought we would be in such a place in our lives?

Now that you have come to believe that there is such a person as Messiah, you will need to know how to think of him. Now that you have placed your undying trust in the word of this Messiah, his word that you can have such a thing as eternal life, you will need to know what that life entails. How can faith in a man dying a tortured death in Jerusalem so long ago have relevance for your life today? How can this reported miracle, of a rabbi who rose from the dead, bring you unwavering security for your future? How can something so feeble and laughable as faith save you from the dangers of this world and beyond?

Be encouraged by the words of an anonymous writer, an apostle who wrote in the first century to a group of Messianic Jewish believers:

3

For you have not come to a tangible mountain, to an ig-
nited fire, to darkness, to murk, to a whirlwind, to the
sound of a shofar [ram's horn], and to a voice whose
words made the hearers beg that no further message be
given to them for they couldn't bear what was being commanded them, "If even a beast touches the mountain, it is
to be stoned to death"; and so terrifying a sight that
Moshe [Moses] said, "I am quaking with dread." On the
contrary, you have come to Mount Tziyon, that is, the city
of the living God, heavenly Yerushalayim [Jerusalem]; to
myriads of angels in festive assembly; to a community of
the firstborn whose names have been recorded in heaven;
to a Judge who is God of everyone; to spirits of righteous
people who have been brought to the goal; to the media-
tor of a new covenant, Yeshua; and to sprinkled blood that
speaks better things than that of Hevel [Abel]. (Heb.
12:18–24)

In short, you have come to a place of glory, a place of security, and
a hope that will never fade away.

What Will You Tell Your Family?

Here is an issue that is a problem for most Jewish believers, as well as new believers from many other backgrounds. Whenever parents or siblings disagree with newfound faith there will be a tension that makes everyone uncomfortable. Some people can handle such tension more easily than others. Some family members will exploit the tension and some will not. There can be no "one size fits all" advice here. A few general principles, however, may save you from barreling into a powder keg.

- Remember the fifth commandment when talking to your parents: Honor your father and mother.
- Do not, at this early stage, let yourself be drawn into an argument or a debate about why you believe.
- Do not talk to your family without first praying and asking for God to grant you courage, peace, and a love for your family.
- Tell them about your newfound faith, but do not expect them to take you very seriously (most family members will hope this is a fad that will pass).
- Be a model of love, of respect, and of resoluteness. Do not get angry at their response, but neither back down from or apologize for your faith.
- Do not try to convince them, as yet, of what you believe.
- Let someone else know that you are going to do this, so that they will be praying for you and so that you will be encouraged by their support (you may need their encouragement to pick you up afterwards).

Parental responses to announcements of newfound faith vary dramatically. I have known families to disown children outright, or to practically disown them by giving them the silent treatment and by making the new believer feel unwelcome at family events. I have heard stories of children being placed in the obituary column, although I have never met anyone who could verify that this happened. Most of the time, nearly without fail, these extreme cases of rejection by family only last a little while. Should this happen to you, remember that with prayer, love, and patience, things are almost certain to get better over time.

A middle-of-the-road reaction is anger and disappointment. Expect this reaction most of the time. Even parents who say, "It's your life; you can believe whatever you want to," rarely mean it. Think about this from their perspective. As you were growing up, they (perhaps) attempted to endow upon you certain values and beliefs. Your newfound faith is a rejection of some of those values. Most people would take such a rejection personally. Understand their anger. Don't allow their anger to create anger in you. Express your continued love for them and assure them that you continue to value their thoughts and feelings. Let them know that a disagreement about God and the meaning of life will not have to separate you as a family.

After you have told your family, a lifetime task begins. Hearing of your faith, they will be watching for hypocrisy and for signs of weakness. Families will usually hope to find opportunities to criticize you and will usually hope to see your faith erode. They'd like to see you return to their values. Be extra cautious and prayerful about your actions and words around family. Your life will speak to them far more than your words about faith ever could.

So when should you speak? Look for teachable moments. Don't cram your faith down their throats. I made that mistake at the age of nineteen. Years later, I still have to tread cautiously on the subject of faith. I have found that resentments for some of my early statements still exist. Look for times when family members are curious or open to hear about your beliefs. Do not speak as an authority, but simply as a believer. Don't imply that they should believe on your authority, but give them reasons for belief that are based upon truth.

I have seen people make the terrible mistake of hiding their faith from their parents. At family reunions they don't bring their Bible (or they hide it). They fearfully attempt to keep involvement in a congregation hidden from parents. Make no mistake, attempting to hide your faith dishonors Yeshua, creates fear in you, and will lead to deeper hurt and resentment later when your faith is discovered.

A friend of mine gave the wisest message I have ever heard on the subject of dealing with family at a Messianic Jewish conference. He read the account of Yeshua's own troubles with family and with hometown folks. After reading the Haftarah (Prophetic) portion at his hometown synagogue, Yeshua found that many were asking how a boy who had grown up in their town could be a man of God. He said, "I tell you that no prophet is accepted in his home town" (Luke 4:24). Even Yeshua's brothers rejected him until after the resurrection. And he was the Messiah! As my friend pointed out, we should not expect to receive better treatment than Yeshua.

How Do You Know That God Accepts You?

There is an enemy of God who wants to cast confusion, doubt, and fear among us. No one knows exactly how he and his minions work. At the very least, it seems that he has promoted certain ideas that work against faith in God. The lie that God will not accept us is one of the most pernicious of the enemy's lies. For most people who struggle with this, the issues are not merely intellectual, but emotional. Nonetheless, it is necessary to deal with the intellectual issue first. Truth must always overrule emotion.

The first antidote to feelings of spiritual unworthiness is a knowledge of God's promises and his unfailing ability to deliver his promises. God's promises are extraordinarily clear in Scripture. In Genesis, God credited righteousness to Abraham because of his faith (Gen. 15:6). At that time he said to Abraham, "Don't be afraid, Avram [Abram]. I am your protector; your reward will be very great" (15:1). Did God follow through on his promise? All the people of Israel today are a testimony of God's promise. Yeshua said, "I AM the Resurrection and the Life! Whoever puts his trust in me will live, even if he dies" (John 11:25). Will he keep that promise? He will as surely as he is God, who cannot lie and who cannot fail. The promises of Yeshua, the prophets, and the apostles about God's blessing of his people are numerous and clear.

The second antidote to feelings of spiritual unworthiness is to get rid of the notion that God's acceptance depends upon you. Who ever said that you had to live up to a standard to be accepted? This is not the message of Yeshua at all. In fact, if you think that God doesn't accept you because of your sinfulness, then you may need to repent and receive his forgiveness. You may not be a believer if you think that the message of Yeshua is, "Be good and I will accept you and give you eternal life." Rather, his message is, "I tell you that whoever hears what I am saying and trusts the one who sent me has eternal life—that is, he will not come up for judgment but has already crossed over from death to life" (John 5:24). Yeshua is the one who saves us. He did not do this because we earned it, but because he wanted to save us. When you stand before God, he will not consider your worthiness as a worshipper to enter heaven, but will accept Yeshua's worthiness as an atonement for you. Yeshua paid the price that your sins deserve with his own body. God's wrath toward you was poured out on him: "But he was wounded because of our crimes, crushed because of our sins; the disciplining that makes us whole fell on him, and by his bruises we are healed" (Isa. 53:5).

These are the intellectual issues. You must know and believe that God accepts you because he promised to, he would not lie, and his acceptance never depended upon you in the first place. The only way God could reject you is if he were a liar and if Yeshua were a failure!

If you have emotional doubts about God's acceptance, let these truths be a rock to you. Stand on the rock of truth when the waves of the sea are crashing around you. The rocks will hold firm against the pounding surf. But there is also another cure for feelings of inadequacy: learn about his great love for you.

The theme of God's love for his creatures is abundant in Scripture. The Jewish prophet Jeremiah said of God's love for Israel, "I love you with an everlasting love; this is why in my grace I draw you to me" (31:3; verse 2 in Jewish Bibles). Jeremiah says this in spite of his repeated indictment of Israel for chasing after idols, whom he refers to as other lovers (3:2, 6–10; 5:7; 9:2; 13:27; 23:10, 14). What kind of God is this who loves even unfaithful subjects?

According to the apostle John, who was the closest of all the disciples to Yeshua, "God is love" (1 John 4:8, 16). Love is the very nature of God. We love because God, who is love, made us and he made us to love. The love you feel for family, for children, for a spouse, for a close friend—all of these loves are little pictures of God's love for you. Yet his love is greater, because we cannot love as perfectly as he does. If your heart is broken when a loved one is hurt, God's is broken all the more at your pain. If you rejoice to see a loved one, God rejoices all the more to spend time with you.

How can you know that God accepts you? Learn and cling to the truth. God promises to accept you and he is no liar. His acceptance is based on Yeshua's worthiness, not yours. And learn about God's loving nature. Rest in his love. Bask in it. If you have never felt loved by anyone, you can feel loved by God. Yeshua's assurance of God's love to his disciples applies to you as well: "For the Father himself loves you, because you have loved me and have believed that I came from God" (John 16:27).

9

What is this New Life About?

I was a college student and a fraternity member. One week I was partying, drinking, and laughing at crude humor with the brothers. The next week, which happened to be the start of a new semester, I was uncomfortable with old habits. I loved my friends at the fraternity, but I didn't enjoy everything we did together. Throwing a Frisbee on the lawn still felt good. Getting drunk and watching many of my friends get high didn't feel so good anymore. What was happening to me?

If you haven't heard yet, you have left an old life and entered a new one. This is especially a favorite concept of the Apostle Paul:

> Therefore, if anyone is united with the Messiah, he is a new creation—the old has passed; look, what has come is fresh and new! (2 Cor. 5:17)

> For neither being circumcised nor being uncircumcised matters; what matters is being a new creation. (Gal. 6:15)

> And clothe yourselves with the new nature created to be godly, which expresses itself in the righteousness and holiness that flow from the truth. (Eph. 4:24)

> . . . and have put on the new self, which is continually being renewed in fuller and fuller knowledge, closer and closer to the image of its Creator. (Col. 3:10)

You still feel like the old you, but in fact, in the spiritual realm, you are completely new. As a matter of fact, you were dead in spirit (Eph. 2:1). You used to be just a body and a soul, but now a new part of you has been born—your spirit. This part of you is alive to God and is a dwelling place for God in your life. At the moment you believed, the Holy Spirit came to dwell in *your* spirit (Eph. 1:13–14). You were born again, which is to say that you were born in the spirit even though you had already been born in the body.

All of this seems confusing at first. In time, you will notice a heightened sensitivity to sin. You will feel a relentless pull toward holiness, purity, and righteousness that was not in your life before. You will find an urge to love people that you would not have even talked to before. All of these are evidence of the spiritual life—and there is more to come. Paul speaks not only of this new self, but also of our old nature. He tells us that we must "put to death" our earthly nature and begin following the impulses of our new nature (Col. 3:5–11). This process will not be automatic. We can't go on cruise control. This will involve resisting temptation to put ourselves (our pleasure, our benefit, our desires, etc.) before others and above God. Little things like lewd conversation, juicy gossip, and wandering eyes are examples of the old life. I needn't mention the larger issues, such as violence, infidelity, fraud, and addiction. God wants us to leave these things behind and to follow our new impulses, which at times will include a desire to pray, to praise God, to tell others about what God has done for us, to share Yeshua with someone else, to encourage someone else, and to read and know his truth found in the Bible.

Become sensitive to this new impulse inside you. Be wary of the excuses and lies of the evil one that will keep you following the old life. All believers are familiar with these excuses: He will forgive me if I sin. I've been doing so well at this lately; I'm sure one slip won't hurt. I'm only human; I can't be expected to resist this!

You will find a new feeling after sin. There will be a lack of peace, which can turn into depression. A major part of your new life will be confessing your wrongdoing to God and asking his forgiveness. On the ultimate level he has already forgiven you. You will not be made to pay the penalty for your sin. But there is another level in which you need forgiveness—the level of day to day relationship. You have become a child of God and your disobedience will not put you out of the family. But it can harm your relationship with him just as disobedience can harm a parent-child relationship.

So how will you adjust to this new life of yours? Make the lifestyle changes that your new impulses are suggesting. Don't even bother grieving over the loss of some of those old, fun habits. They will be replaced by something much better. Make the most of worshipful moments with God. Take advantage of the Bible as the source of spiritual knowledge. Talk to God frequently, not just on your knees but throughout the day no matter what you are doing. As I have discovered, and so many others have as well, the new life beats the old one hands down.

What is this Immersion or *Tvilah* About?

Immersion has a long history amongst the Jewish people. Immersion in and washings in water were a part of the practice of ancient Israel. One of the great vessels in the ancient Tabernacle (which later became the Temple) was a basin of bronze in which fresh water was kept. Priests entering the sanctuary or approaching the altar were required to wash their hands and feet (Exod. 40:30–32). Those who were ritually unclean due to a skin disease had to finish their purification with a bath (Lev. 14:8). By the first century, immersion in water for purification was a common ritual. The people at Qumran, who wrote the Dead Sea Scrolls, immersed themselves daily for purification. The Pharisees, a fraternity of pious men, emphasized ritual handwashings as an important part of religion. Gentile converts to Judaism were required to undergo ritual immersion in water before the first century.

This Jewish practice of washing with water is very much alive today in the Orthodox community. Women who have waited seven days from the end of their menstrual cycle must bathe thoroughly at home and then come to the *mikveh*, or immersion pool, of their local synagogue for a ritual immersion. The purpose of the *mikveh* is symbolic purification, not physical washing. Modern Gentile converts to Judaism are still required to go to the *mikveh*.

In light of the long history of immersion in and washing with water, the people of Israel in the first century were not surprised by the methods of a wandering prophet named John. John the Baptist, as he is commonly known, came to the people with a message from God to prepare for the coming of his kingdom. John called on people to repent, which means to turn *away* from sins and *toward* godly things. He required those who would make such a commitment to be immersed in water at the Jordan River. Yeshua himself went out to John to be immersed, even though John protested (Matt. 3). John knew that Yeshua was the one he had proclaimed who would come and usher in God's kingdom.

Yeshua commanded that this ritual immersion in water continue. After he had risen from the dead, when he was physically leaving this world and ascending into heaven to sit at God's right hand, Yeshua said: "Therefore, go and make people from all nations into *talmidim* [disciples], immersing them into the reality of the Father, the Son, and the *Ruach HaKodesh* [Holy Spirit]"

13

(Matt. 28:19). The apostles immediately began following this practice. In his very first sermon, Peter said to those in the crowd who wanted to follow the teachings of Yeshua: "Turn from sin, return to God, and each of you be immersed on the authority of Yeshua the Messiah into forgiveness of sins, and you will receive the gift of the *Ruach HaKodesh*" (Acts 2:38). Peter and the disciples immersed 3,000 Jewish people that day!

In spite of all of this history and of the Jewishness of ritual immersion in water, baptism has historically been a problem for the Jewish people. During a large part of history, the dominant church in Europe used baptism as a means to "convert" Jewish people to Christianity. The idea was that a baptized Jewish man or woman was no longer Jewish. To the Jewish community, baptism came to symbolize a rejection of all things Jewish. Even today, some Jewish parents can bear seeing their child come to faith in Yeshua as the Messiah, but they beg their children not to be baptized. This sad history of baptism explains why most Messianic Jews prefer to use terms like "immersion" or *tvilah*, rather than "baptism."

In light of this fact, what is the right thing to do? If you have not already been immersed, should you? Will you be rejecting your Jewish heritage to do so? As is always the case, truth matters more than appearances. Immersion is not a rejection of Jewish heritage, but is a part of that heritage. More importantly, Yeshua's commandment that you should be immersed is of the utmost importance.

Immersion for believers in Yeshua is a symbolic act just like the washings required of the priests in the days of the Temple. The priestly washings symbolized purity, so that no contamination would be brought to the altar or into the sanctuary. *Tvilah* in Yeshua is symbolic both of entering the community of believers and of the death, burial, and resurrection of Yeshua (Rom. 6:4). As we are buried under the water and raised, we become a picture of his burial and resurrection. If you properly understand the ceremony, it is a beautiful picture. *Tvilah* is also an opportunity to express our love for Messiah by obeying him. As he said to his disciples, "If you love me, you will keep my commands" (John 14:15).

Section

BEGINNING STEPS

Two

Introduction

Within this section there are seven studies dealing with issues that are basic to the beginning of life in Yeshua. The best way to use these studies is in conjunction with another believer, who is mature in the faith, and who can discuss these issues with you and add his or her own experiences and values (see "How To Use This Book").

At the end of each study, there are five daily assignments. Doing these assignments during the week will add tremendously to the value of the studies. Some daily assignments may review issues raised in previous studies and others will look ahead to upcoming studies.

The Basics of Faith

Key Verse: "He believed in ADONAI, and he credited it to him as righteousness." (Gen. 15:6)

Illustrating the Issue

All the eyes then looking were fixed upon the Nazarene. It may have been pity with which he was moved. Whatever the cause, Ben-Hur was conscious of a change in his feelings. A conception of something better than the best of this life—something so much better that it could serve a weak man with strength to endure the agonies of spirit as well as of body, something to make death welcome—perhaps another life purer than this one, perhaps the spirit life which Balthasar held to so fast—began to dawn upon his mind clearer and clearer, bringing to him a certain sense that, after all, the mission of the Nazarene was that of guide across the boundary for such as loved him, across the boundary to where his kingdom was set up and waiting for him. Then, as something borne through the air, out of the almost forgotten, he heard again, or seemed to hear, the saying of the Nazarene:

"I am the Resurrection and the Life."

And the words repeated themselves over and over, and took form, and the dawn touched them with its light and filled them with a new meaning. And as men repeat a question to grasp and fix the meaning, he asked, gazing at the figure on the hill fainting under its crown, Who the Resurrection? And who the Life?

"I AM"

the figure seemed to say—and say it for him, for instantly he was sensible of a peace such as he had never known—the peace which is the end of doubt and mystery, and the beginning of faith and love and clear understanding.[1]

Check the box that best applies:
❑ I am certain that I have eternal life.
❑ I am reasonably certain that I have eternal life.
❑ I will be certain that I have eternal life if I can live a good life.
❑ I am not really sure there is such a thing as eternal life.

Check the answer that seems most correct:
❑ Faith is believing without evidence.
❑ Faith is blind trust.
❑ Faith is believing God about things we cannot know on our own.
❑ Faith is hoping for the things we want to believe.
❑ Faith is knowing for sure the things we can prove.

Getting God's Perspective: Read Ephesians 2:8–9.
Note: Grace means "undeserved favor." To receive grace is to be given something good that we did not earn.

What does it mean to be "saved" or "delivered"? _____
_____

How does Paul say that we have been "saved" or "delivered"?
_____
_____

If our salvation were based upon good deeds, what would we be prone to do? _____
_____

Do you know anyone who is trying to earn salvation by his good deeds? Who? _____
_____

Which seems harder, being saved by faith or by good deeds? Why?
_____
_____
_____
_____

19

A Deeper Look

Some people think that in the days of Moses, keeping the *Torah* saved people and that Yeshua and the apostles changed the basis of salvation to faith. But actually, The *Torah* and the Prophets did not speak often about eternal salvation. They mostly taught about living for God in this life. However, we do get some hints of their view of salvation, as in Genesis 15:6: "He believed in *ADONAI*, and he credited it to him as righteousness." This was said of Abraham, who lived about 600 years before Moses.

Why did God credit righteousness to Abraham? _____

_____

What did Abraham have to do to be considered righteous by God?

_____

_____

Most people think that all people go to heaven except for really bad people. Some people are stricter and think that only good people go to heaven. What many do not realize is that God's standard for what is good is much higher than our own. Solomon expresses this in Proverbs 20:9: "Who can say, 'I have made my heart clean, I am cleansed from sin'?" David says this in Psalm 14:3: "But all turn aside, all alike are corrupt; no one does what is right, not a single one."

According to Solomon and David, what are a person's chances who expects God to let them into heaven because they were good?

_____

_____

Abraham was deemed righteous by God because he believed God's promise. God's promise to all people today is very specific. He promises eternal life to those who believe in the person and work of the Messiah. Paul has this to say about the person and work of Messiah: "For while we were still helpless, at the right time, the Messiah died on behalf of ungodly people . . . Therefore, since we have now come to be considered righteous by means of his bloody sacrificial death, how much more will we be delivered through him from the anger of God's judgment" (Rom. 5:6, 9).

What did Yeshua do to make us righteous in God's eyes? _____

_____

What must we do to be made righteous in God's eyes? _____

_____

While Paul says in Ephesians 2:8–9 that we are saved by faith and not by good deeds, he tells the rest of the story in Ephesians 2:10, the very next verse: "For we are of God's making, created in union with Messiah Yeshua for a life of good actions already prepared by God for us to do." While the basis of our salvation is faith, not good deeds, the *result* of our salvation will be good deeds. We will be motivated to obey God, not to earn his favor, but because we have already received his favor.

How would you respond to a critic who said, "This idea of faith in Yeshua means that people can just sin all they want to and still go to heaven"? _____

_____

_____

Homework

Day 1: Memorize Eph. 2:8–9.
Day 2: Review Eph. 2:8–9 and read Dan. 12:1–2.
Day 3: Memorize Gen. 15:6 and review Eph. 2:8–9.
Day 4: Review Gen. 15:6 and read John 3:10–21.
Day 5: Read John 5:19–47 and review Gen. 15:6 and Eph. 2:8–9.

Who Is This God We Worship?

Key Verse: "For indeed, 'Our God is a consuming fire!'"
(Heb. 12:29)

Illustrating the Issue

A non-Jew asked Rabbi Joshua ben Korcha, "Why did God choose to speak to Moses through a [common] thorn bush? [Why not out of a greater tree?]"

The rabbi answered, "Were it a carob tree or a sycamore tree, you would have asked the same question, but to dismiss you without any reply is not right, so I will tell you why. To teach us that there is no place devoid of God's presence, not even a thorn bush."[2]

Check the view of God which has most influenced you in the past:
❏ God is a cosmic party-pooper, punishing anyone who has fun.
❏ God is all sweetness and love, forgiving and loving.
❏ God is all wrath and holiness, punishing and cursing.
❏ God does not fit in a box. He is both just and loving and does not answer to us.
❏ God is another name for the laws of nature, by which the universe runs.
❏ God is the force of life in all things and we all are part of God.
❏ God made the universe, but he doesn't pay us any attention now.

Check the box that best applies:
❏ I am learning to trust God to meet all of my needs.
❏ I am having trouble learning to trust God.
❏ I'm not sure God can be trusted that far.

Getting God's Perspective: Read Isaiah 40:10–25.

How is the picture of God in verse 11 different than the picture in verse 17? _____

_____

_____

Why is it important to you for God to be a tender shepherd over you? _____

_____

Why is it important to you for God to be a ruler over the whole earth? _____

_____

What is the main message that Isaiah is preaching here about God?

_____

_____

A Deeper Look

Many people do not have a balanced view of God. According to the Bible, God is both far and near and he is both just and loving. God is far above us, which theologians call transcendence, and he is near to us, which is imminence. This is not a paradox, but rather it means that the greatest and highest being in the universe comes near to us, seeking a relationship. God is just and punishes sinful thoughts and deeds, but he is also loving and ready to forgive: ". . . showing grace to the thousandth generation, forgiving offenses, crimes and sins; yet not exonerating the guilty, but causing the negative effects of the parents' offenses to be experienced by their children and grandchildren, and even by the third and fourth generations" (Exod. 34:7). If God were near to us but not above us, we wouldn't respect him. If God were far above us but not near to us, we wouldn't love him. If he were just and unloving, we would only fear him; if loving but unjust we would have no relief from the violence of the wicked.

What did God's justice require of you in order for you to receive eternal life? _____

_____

_____

23

What did God's justice require of Yeshua for you to receive eternal life? _____

_____

    God has many attributes. He is holy, which means that he is completely separate from evil and wickedness. He is omniscient (all-knowing), omnipotent (all-powerful), and omnipresent (all-present). He is eternal and infinite, yet personal and loving. He is faithful and just, yet forgiving and kind. He also exists as a Tri-Unity (or a Trinity): Father, Son, and Spirit. Originally he revealed himself only as one, probably because of idolatry. If he had revealed his Tri-Unity, the Israelites may have misunderstood and worshipped three Gods. We only know of his Tri-Unity because of the teaching of the Bible. The Hebrew Scriptures allowed for this Tri-Unity (some would even say hinted at it) while the New Testament teaches it more clearly.

In John 10:30, during the Hanukkah celebration at the Temple in Jerusalem, Yeshua said, "I and the Father are one." Who was Yeshua claiming to be? _____

In Acts 5:3, Peter says that Ananias (Hananyah) lied to the Holy Spirit. In verse 4, Peter says, "You have lied not to human beings, but to God!" Who is the Holy Spirit? _____

_____

In John 8:19, Yeshua says, "You know neither me nor my Father; if you knew me, you would know my Father too." Who is the Father? _____

    Many great thinkers have considered how God can be one and yet three. The best answer anyone has been able to give is that God is one being, who is so complex that his being exists in three different persons. Other explanations have been considered, such as the idea that God sometimes is the Father, sometimes the Son, and sometimes the Spirit. But views like this do not explain the evidence in the Bible. Below is a chart which describes the best answer that humans can conceive for the meaning of the Triune nature of God:

24

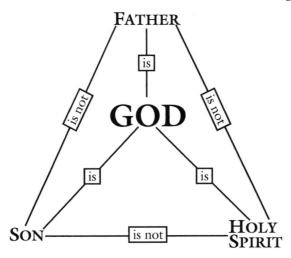

Homework

Day 1: Review Eph. 2:8–9 and Gen. 15:6. Read John 14:8–14.
Day 2: Memorize John 1:1.
Day 3: Review John 1:1 and memorize John 1:14.
Day 4: Review John 1:1 and John 1:14. Read 2 Tim. 3:16–17.
Day 5: Read Ps. 119.

Getting to Know God in Scripture

Key Verse: "Make me understand the way of your precepts, and I will meditate on your wonders." (Ps. 119:27)

Illustrating the Issue

A poor man, a rich man, and a wicked man presented themselves before the heavenly tribunal. The poor man was asked, "Why did you not occupy yourself with *Torah*?" If he answer that he was poverty-stricken and worried about his sustenance, then it is said to him, "Were you poorer than Hillel?" It is related of Hillel the Elder that for his daily work he only earned half a denarius; but he gave half of it to the doorkeeper of the house of study for admission and spent the remainder on supporting himself and the members of his household. On one occasion he was without work and earned nothing, and the doorkeeper refused to admit him. So he climbed up and sat outside the window in order to hear the words of the living God expounded by Shemaya and Abtalion. Tradition has it that the day referred to was the eve of Sabbath in midwinter and snow fell heavily. At the break of dawn Shemaya said to Abtalion, "My colleague, usually the room is light, but to-day it is dark; perhaps it is cloudy." Then they looked up at the window and saw the form of a man. They went out and found him covered with three cubits of snow.[3]

Check the view that has most influenced your life before knowing Yeshua:
❑ The Bible is a fairy tale.
❑ The Bible is a book written by men about God.
❑ The Bible is a book written by God about men.
❑ The Bible is inspired by God and is true in all that it says.
❑ The Bible is inspired by God just as any good religious book is.
❑ The Bible is full of contradictions.
❑ The Bible is the only reliable source of information about who God is.

Getting God's Perspective: Read Psalm 119:97–104

Describe the Psalmist's attitude toward the Torah. _____

_____

What are some of the benefits that the Psalmist derived from reading the Torah? _____

_____

In verse 102, the Psalmist says, "you have instructed me." What does this imply about the Torah? _____

_____

According to verse 97, how consistent and frequent is the Psalmist's meditation upon the teachings of God? _____

_____

_____

A Deeper Look

For some people the idea of a Bible that is inspired by God sounds ridiculous. But ask yourself this question: How can we know about God unless he tells us about himself? If you believe that God exists and if you have noticed that he doesn't show himself in plain view, then you can see that God must have some other way to let us know about him. He could have spoken directly to each one of us, but hasn't chosen to. He could have spoken directly to a prophet like Mohammed and given us his direct words. But he chose to do something more complicated, something that takes more faith to believe in. He did sometimes speak directly through prophets, but for the most part, he inspired men to write about him in their own words. The writings of these men contain perfect truth about God because God directed their writing with an unseen hand: "for never has a prophecy come as a result of human willing—on the contrary, people moved by the *Ruach HaKodesh* [Holy Spirit] spoke a message from God" (2 Pet. 1:21).

How do you feel about the Bible? Uncertain? Sure it is God's book? Not sure but open to read it and learn? _____

_____

_____

27

There are a variety of ways to obtain knowledge, inspiration, and wisdom from the Bible. No one of these ways is better or more important that the others. Those who would get the most from the Bible will use a variety of these means. For each person, however, there will be methods that work better than others and which will become favorites.

1. Hearing God's Word: This may be from sermons heard live, on the radio, or on tapes. The Scriptures can also be purchased on tapes and other media.

2. Reading God's Word: Rather than focusing on individual verses or small sections like the remaining methods, simply reading the Bible involves learning whole books and large sections.

3. Memorizing God's Word: Usually this will involve memorizing one verse at a time, although some like to memorize chapters. This will give you insight as you repeat the verse again and again; it will also enable you to carry the verses with you wherever you go.

4. Meditating on God's Word: By carrying a verse or small section of Scripture with you and meditating on it throughout the day or by simply spending some time repeating verses over and over, you can gain tremendous insight.

5. Praying God's Word: Many parts of the Bible are prayers, especially in the Psalms. Other parts can be easily modified into prayers. This will help you put the language of Scripture into your prayers.

6. Studying God's Word: This involves taking sections of the Bible and researching the meaning of words, finding parallel passages on the same topic, researching the historical background, and determining the meaning intended by the writer for a given passage.

Which of these methods immediately looks to you like the one you would choose? _____

For most of us, the truth is that God is not going to speak with us directly. Only a few in history have had that privilege. The

Bible is God's most direct voice in our lives. Below is a breakdown of the types of books in the Bible[4] and a general idea of how God speaks to us in them.

The Five Books of the Torah:
These contain history and commandments. The history shows us God in action. We learn about him like discovering a character in a novel. The commandments show us God's priorities. In these books there are some commandments that are no longer in effect. Usually these have to do with ceremonial and sacrificial issues. Although we no longer keep these commandments, they teach us something about God's holiness.

The Historical Books:
These are a part of the *Nevi'im* or Prophetic Books in the Jewish Bible. They include Joshua, Judges, Samuel, and Kings, as well as several books found in the *Ketuvim* (Writings) in the Jewish Bible: Chronicles, Ezra, Nehemiah, and Esther. These show us God in action.

The Poetic and Wisdom Books:
Poetry, like in Psalms, is often prayer and praise to God. Wisdom, like Job, Proverbs, Ecclesiastes, and Song of Solomon, shows us practical insight for daily living.

The Prophetic Books:
These books focus on four kinds of teaching. There are prophecies of judgment, showing the justice of God in punishing sin, cruelty, and rebellion. There are prophecies of indictment, showing what attitudes and actions God regards as sin. There are prophecies of the restoration of Israel, which give us a future hope and show God's power to overcome evil. And there are prophecies of instruction, in which God tells us how to live.

The Gospels:
These are like four biographical portraits of Yeshua. They are each written with different perspectives and showing different aspects of Yeshua.

The Epistles (Letters):
These include all of the books from Romans to Jude. These books are letters from the apostles answering questions and addressing issues raised in the early congregations. They often teach direct tenets of the faith and give practical wisdom to believers.

Revelation:
This book stands alone and is related to certain passages in Ezekiel, Daniel, and Zechariah which speak symbolically about the events at the end of our age. This book presents a message of hope and victory for the kingdom of Messiah.

Which section of the Bible interests you the most at this point? _

Homework

Day 1: Review Eph. 2:8–9 and Gen. 15:6. Read 2 Tim. 3:16–17.
Day 2: Review John 1:1 and John 1:14. Read Ps. 19.
Day 3: Memorize 2 Tim. 3:16–17.
Day 4: Review 2 Tim. 3:16–17. Read Psalm 5:1–4.
Day 5: Read Matt. 14:23; 26:36; Mark 1:35; and Luke 9:18.

Meeting God in Prayer

Key Verse: "But you, when you pray, go into your room, close the door, and pray to your Father in secret. Your Father, who sees what is done in secret, will reward you." (Matt. 6:6)

Illustrating the Issue

After the war I tried again to travel abroad, but the army wouldn't give a permit for more than two weeks. So I finally decided to travel around Israel instead and enjoy our beautiful country. I took a backpack and a sleeping bag and set off to explore the length and breadth of our little land. My first stop was at the Lake of Galilee. On the beach there I met a young English girl, Henny. I was immediately attracted to her at that first meeting because there was something different about her . . . She had this special relationship with God, very direct and personal. She would talk to him freely as to a friend. She claimed that he gave her guidance and direction. It all seemed very strange to me. I decided she had a powerful imagination and that she assumed her subconscious wishes were God's will.[5]

Check all views of prayer that you have held at any time in your life:
- ❏ Prayer is chanting or saying aloud written prayers.
- ❏ Prayer is chanting or saying aloud written prayers in another language.
- ❏ Prayer is when you talk to yourself.
- ❏ Prayer is conversation between God and myself.
- ❏ Prayer is for meals and bedtime.
- ❏ Prayer is only for times when people are gathered for worship.
- ❏ Prayer can involve the use of written prayers or it can be an expression of my thoughts to God.
- ❏ Prayer is telling God all the things I want him to do.
- ❏ Prayer is an intimate relationship between God and me.
- ❏ Prayer is something you do when you want to appear religious.

Getting God's Perspective: Read Matt. 6:5–13.

Why do you think it is hypocritical to pray in order to be seen by others? _____

_____

Does this mean that all public prayer is forbidden? Why or why not? _____

_____

Why would it be important to God that we pray in secret? _____

_____

_____

Pagan babbling in prayer, mentioned in verse 7, involved the use of many manipulative and insincere statements. Pagans believed that short prayers were an offense and that multitudes of praises should be put into prayers and that the one praying should demean himself frequently. By doing this, they hoped to stir the egos of the gods to get them to listen. Why won't this work on God?

_____

_____

Verses 9–13 are known as the "Lord's Prayer" or the "Disciples' Prayer." Look at the pronouns. Who is praying? _____

Why do you think the Lord's Prayer uses plural pronouns? _____

_____

Exactly what sort of things are we asking for if we pray the Lord's Prayer? _____

_____

_____

A Deeper Look

There are several different subjects that we ought to bring up to God in prayer:

1. Praise: Taking time to glorify God by praising his attributes. For example, "Oh God, you are more loving than anyone and you have shown us your love in Yeshua."
2. Thanksgiving: This is thanking him for what he has done in our lives. For example, "Father, thank you for allowing me to show my love to my children today. I thank you for giving each one of them to me."
3. Confession: This is admitting our sins to God and asking his forgiveness. For example, "Lord, I know that I was wrong to react in selfish anger to my boss today. Please forgive me and teach me patience with my tongue."
4. Petition: This is asking for our own needs and desires. For example, "Father, if it is your will, I ask that you give me favor in the eyes of my employer today."
5. Intercession: This is asking God for the needs of others. For example, "Lord, may you give strength to Steven right now and lead him to say the right words to his father."

Which of these subjects of prayer have you used recently? _____
_____

There is no one way to pray. Nor should we all pray just one way. A variety of different types of prayer are helpful for everyone. Below is a partial list of types of prayer:

1. Reading prewritten prayers, such as from the Psalms or a prayer-book (*siddur*), is one way to pray. This has the advantage of uniting the one who is praying with the rest of the Jewish people.
2. Praying alone in your bedroom or another private place and bringing many subjects of prayer to God is another kind. Many people do this at least once a day and consider it to be the mainstay of their prayer life.
3. Talking to God either in your head or softly out loud throughout the day is another important kind of prayer. You can talk to him like a friend, remembering that he is also your King.
4. Getting together with other believers for group prayer or praying together with a spouse out loud is another type.

5. Prayer walks can be very helpful. Just take a walk and pray to God in your head as you go. Some people like to pray for the people that they pass by as they walk.

What methods of prayer have you used recently? _____
_____

Homework

Day 1: Pray alone for 15 minutes.
Day 2: Review Eph. 2:8–9; Gen. 15:6; John 1:1 and 1:14.
Day 3: Try a prayer walk for at least 15 minutes.
Day 4: Pray some prewritten prayers, such as the *Amidah* or Psalm 23.
Day 5: Read Col. 1:14–23. Try talking to God throughout the day, wherever you are.

Who Is This Savior?

Key Verse: "And when he appeared as a human being, he humbled himself still more by becoming obedient even to death—death on the stake as a criminal!" (Phil. 2:8)

Illustrating the Issue

Then comes the real shock. Among those Jews there suddenly turns up a man who goes about talking as if he is God. He claims to forgive sins. He says he has always existed. He says he is coming to judge the world at the end of time. Now let us get this clear. Among pantheists, like the Indians, anyone might say that he is part of God, or one with God: there would be nothing very odd about it. But this man, since he was a Jew, could not mean that kind of God. God, in their language, meant the Being outside of the world who made it and was infinitely different from anything else. And, when you have grasped that, you will see that what this man said was, quite simply, the most shocking thing that has ever been uttered by human lips. . . .

I am trying here to prevent anyone from saying the really foolish thing that people often say about him: "I'm ready to accept Jesus as a great moral teacher, but I don't accept his claim to be God." That is the one thing we must not say. A man who was merely a man and said the things that Jesus said would not be a great moral teacher. He would either be a lunatic—on a level with a man who says that he is a poached egg—or else he would be the Devil of hell. You must make your choice. Either this man was and is the Son of God: or else a madman and something worse. You can shut him up for a fool, you can spit at him and kill him as a demon; or you can fall at his feet and call him Lord and God. But let us not come with any patronizing nonsense about him being a great human teacher. He has not left that open to us. He has not intended to.[6]

35

Who do you think Yeshua is?
❑ The Creator of the Universe
❑ The Judge of all Mankind
❑ The Head of all Congregations
❑ The Beginning and the End
❑ As much human as you and I
❑ The Messiah of Israel and the Nations
❑ The Coming King
❑ The Prince of Peace
❑ The God of the Universe
❑ All of the above

Getting God's Perspective: Read Hebrews 2:9–18.

The writer says that Yeshua "was made for a little while lower than the angels." This implies that Yeshua was above the angels at some point. When was Yeshua above the angels? _____
_____

Verse 14 says that Yeshua "became like them and shared that human nature." What nature did Yeshua have before he became a man? _____

How did he "taste death for everyone"? _____
_____

According to verse 14, was Yeshua as fully human as you and I?
_____

How does the fact of Yeshua's suffering in verse 18 make him better fit to help us? _____
_____
_____

A Deeper Look

Before Yeshua became a man he was God: ". . . the Word was God. . . . The Word became a human being and lived with us" (John 1:1, 14). After Yeshua became a man he was just as human as you and I: "This is why he had to become like his brothers in every respect—so that he might become a merciful and faithful *cohen gadol* [High Priest] in the service of God, making a *kapparah* [atonement] for the sins of the people" (Heb. 2:17). Yeshua did not, however, cease to be God while he was with us as a man. Yeshua was a bridge between man and God. He had to be fully human or his sacrifice wouldn't have reached down to our level. He had to be fully divine or his sacrifice wouldn't have been of enough value to merit forgiveness for all time and all believers.

What is the hardest thing for you to understand about Yeshua being human and divine at the same time? _____
_____

In the history of faith in Yeshua, there have been a number of erroneous views about his human and divine nature. In one view, called Apollinarianism, it was thought that Yeshua had merely held a human body but had no human soul. His human body was made alive by God's Spirit inside.

If Apollinarianism were true, why wouldn't Yeshua have been fully human? _____
_____

In the view called Adoptionism, Yeshua was merely a man until his immersion, when the Spirit came upon him. At that point he was united with God and became the God-man.

If Adoptionism were true, why wouldn't Yeshua have been fully divine? _____
_____

The Scriptures do not directly address the issue of how Yeshua was divine and human at the same time. Rather, some Scriptures affirm that he was human and some that he was divine. Furthermore, Yeshua said to Philip, "Whoever has seen me has seen the Father" (John 14:9). Yeshua was divine even when he was human. Theologians call this the hypostatic union. Both his humanity and his divinity were real at the same time. I heard a preacher once say it even better: he was the only 200% man who ever lived—100% human and 100% divine at the same time.

Was Yeshua a man who became God or God who became a man? What is the difference? _____

_____

Yeshua existed before he was born as God the Son. He dwells now, still with his body, at the right hand of God the Father. Because Yeshua was God before he became a man, Paul can say that "in connection with him were created all things . . . they have all been created through him and for him" (Col. 1:16).

Have you ever considered Yeshua the Creator before? How does it make you feel to know that your Savior is also your Creator? ___

_____

_____

Homework

Day 1: Review Eph. 2:8–9; Gen. 15:6; John 1:1 and 14.
Day 2: Read Phil. 2:6–11.
Day 3: Meditate on Col. 1:16 (repeat it again and again to yourself, thinking of its meaning).
Day 4: Read 1 Cor. 12:4–30.
Day 5: Memorize Heb. 10:25.

Who Needs a Congregation?

Key Verses: "And let us keep paying attention to one another, in order to spur each other on to love and good deeds, not neglecting our own congregational meetings, as some have made a practice of doing, but, rather, encouraging each other. And let us do this all the more as you see the day approaching." (Heb. 10:24–25)

Illustrating the Issue

In the following story, Ricardo is a transvestite addicted to crack cocaine, who came to know Messiah through the loving witness of a local congregation.

I will never forget the Tuesday night we introduced him to the congregation. He stood before us, a bit shy, in male clothing. His blond hair had been cut, and dark roots were now growing out. His nail polish had been chipped off. Subconscious habits were being overhauled with instruction from Terry and others: "No, Ricardo, don't cross your legs like that. Put your ankle all the way up on your other knee. . . ." It sounds humorous, but they had to start all the way back at "square one" with how a man sits and walks.

The congregation couldn't help but cheer and praise God for this miracle. Ricardo stood there perplexed at the noise. Why were these people applauding him?

In the months that followed, Ricardo made great progress in his spiritual life. It took three months to get him straight enough to even be accepted in a drug rehabilitation program. Nevertheless, his commitment to follow Christ was solid. The old had gone, the new had definitely come.

Ricardo had come out of pitch blackness and into the light. Charles Spurgeon [a famous preacher] once said that when a jeweler shows his best diamonds, he sets them against a black velvet backdrop. The contrast of the jewels against the dark velvet brings out the luster. In the same way, God does his most stunning work where things seem hopeless. Wherever there is pain, suffering, and desperation, Jesus is. And that's where his people belong—among those who are vulnerable, who think nobody cares.[7]

What is a congregation?
❏ A building where God's presence dwells
❏ A group of people worshipping, learning and serving the Messiah
❏ A religious club where meetings are held
❏ A school to learn the Bible
❏ A house of prayer

Getting God's Perspective: Read Acts 2:42–47.

What four things is this congregation devoted to? _____
_____

The apostles, called "emissaries" in the *Complete Jewish Bible,* were the first leaders of the congregations. Why would a congregation study their teaching? _____
_____

Is the teaching of the apostles available to us today in any form?
_____
_____

What value might there be in fellowship between members of the congregation? How would that serve Yeshua? _____
_____

The term "breaking bread" refers to meals shared between believers. Why is it important for believers to do things together, such as sharing meals? _____
_____

This early congregation prayed together. What benefit is there in praying as a group? _____
_____

Can these four practices of the early Jerusalem congregation be done just as well alone? Why or why not? _____

_____

According to verse 46, how often were these people together? Why do you think Luke felt it important to include this information in Acts?_____

_____

What is the last line of verse 47 about? _____

_____

A Deeper Look

The early Jerusalem congregation is held up by Luke, the author of Acts, as an example of God's will for a congregation. The power of the example is not in the specifics. Meeting daily in the Temple courts, for example, is no longer possible. The importance of the example is in the power and value of this community of faith. These people prayed together, learned Scripture together, shared meals, fellowshipped, and witnessed together. They cared for the needs of each other, in this case even going so far as to share their possessions when needed. They became a family.

Are you experiencing this type of family at your congregation? Explain._____

_____

_____

A congregation is the people, not the place. The word used in Greek in the New Testament is *ekklesia*, which means an assembly. No special emphasis is given to the place where people meet. The early congregations met in homes. The Jerusalem congregation also met together every day in the Temple courts. What is emphasized about the congregation is what it does together: prayer, musical worship, hearing and teaching the Scriptures, remembering Messiah's death and resurrection, taking the message of Yeshua to those not in the congregation, and fellowshipping together as a family of faith.

41

Paul compares the congregation to a body: "Now you together constitute the body of the Messiah, and individually you are parts of it" (1 Cor. 12:27). The term "Body of Messiah" is often used of all believers in the whole world as a group. Each local congregation is also a local "Body of Messiah." The analogy to the body is simple: interconnectedness. Parts of a body all need each other and perform many different functions. No function is dispensable. You may not know your function in the body now, but you must be open to find a place. Other believers will help you to see how you can fit in. Pray for God to show you.

Some parts of the body regulate other parts. The head, according to Paul, is Yeshua. Below him, but over many other parts of the body, are various kinds of leaders: pastors and teachers. Other terms such as elder, minister, shepherd, or even leader may be used. In some Messianic Jewish congregations, the term "rabbi" is used, though not all agree that this is a proper term.[8] These leaders in various roles are to serve the body by giving an example, not merely by giving orders. Yeshua modeled such servant leadership when he washed the feet of the disciples (John 13).

How does the picture of the congregation as a body strike you? What is there about a body that makes it such a good analogy for a congregation? _____

_____

All of the members of a congregation have a responsibility toward one another. The modern idea that a worship service is a spectator event is not found in Scripture. Paul says to the believers in Colossae, "Let the Word of Messiah, in all its richness, live in you, as you teach and counsel one another in all wisdom, and as you sing psalms, hymns, and spiritual songs with gratitude to God in your hearts" (Col. 3:16). All members are to be involved in the lives of other members, as a kind of extended family, teaching and counseling one another in love.

Have you already been experiencing this in your congregation? Explain. _____

_____

42

The work of some chosen leaders in the congregation is to be supported financially by the members (1 Tim. 5:17–18). Other work of the congregation is also to be supported on the principle that "he who plants sparingly also harvests sparingly" (2 Cor. 9:6). In other words, if you want to share in the rewards that God will bestow for the work of the congregation, then you must support the work. The more you support the work with your participation and your finances, the more your portion of God's reward will be.

Have you made plans to support your congregation? _____

Homework

Day 1: Review Eph. 2:8–9; Gen. 15:6; John 1:1 and 14.

Day 2: Read Eph. 4:1–16.

Day 3: Review Heb. 10:25.

Day 4: Memorize Matt. 28:19.

Day 5: Read Acts 4:1–20.

Sharing Your Story With Others

Key Verses: "Therefore go and make people from all nations into *talmidim* [disciples], immersing them into the reality of the Father, the Son, and the *Ruach HaKodesh* [Holy Spirit], and teaching them to obey everything that I have commanded you." (Matt. 28:19–20)

Illustrating the Issue

Odessa Moore, a Prison Fellowship volunteer and member of the Faithful Central Missionary Baptist Church in South Central Los Angeles, is a good example.

Eight years ago when Odessa was visiting the juvenile jail, she met a teenager waiting to be tried as an adult for first-degree murder. His eyes chilled her, they were so full of hate and anger.

"I don't care about anything," he said defiantly. "I don't feel no shame."

A familiar story emerged as they talked—father a drug user, mother an alcoholic, both parents abusive. They would beat the boy and tie him up in the closet for hours. All of his life he had been told that he was nothing. No one cared about him. But that was all right, he said.

"I don't care about nobody."

"There is someone who loves you," Odessa told him.

"No way," he responded. "Nobody."

"You're in here for murder, right?" asked Odessa.

"Yes, and I'd do it again," he said.

"How would you like it if someone came in here tonight and said, 'I know you've committed murder and they're going to give you the death penalty, but I am going to take your place for you.' How would you like that?"

For the first time the boy showed a spark of life. "Are you kidding? That would be great!"

Odessa went on to tell him about Jesus, the prisoner who did take his place, who had already paid the price for his wrongdoing. Using word pictures the young man could understand—he had obviously never heard anything about the gospel—she walked him through the steps to a growing understanding of sin, repentance, forgiveness, and freedom—true freedom—in Christ. [9]

How do you feel about talking to other people about faith in Yeshua?
❏ That sounds too hard for me
❏ I have already been doing it, but I'd like to know more
❏ "Proselytizing" is not a Jewish thing to do
❏ Yeshua commanded that we tell others and I want to learn how

Getting God's Perspective: Read Acts 8:26–39

Was Philip sent out into the desert just at random or for a reason? Explain. _____

_____

What was God's heart for the Ethiopian? How can you tell? ____

_____

According to verse 35, how did Philip tell the Ethiopian about Yeshua? _____

_____

What Scripture passage was the Ethiopian reading? _____

_____

How would you summarize the message that Philip got across to the Ethiopian? _____

_____

A Deeper Look

The simplest thing that you have to share with others is your own story. Many believers refer to this as your "testimony." David practiced this when he frequently told others about the things God had done in his life: "All day long my mouth will tell of your righteous deeds and acts of salvation" (Ps. 71:15).

Briefly write down or tell someone else the story of your coming
to faith in Yeshua. _____

_____

_____

_____

_____

_____

_____

_____

Remember when sharing about Yeshua with others that it is
important to be natural. Those who do not yet believe in Yeshua
sometimes stereotype believers as "brainwashed" or "out of
touch." Try not to use religious words that other people might
not understand, unless you explain them (such as "salvation,"
"born again," or "grace"). Most importantly, remember that we
cannot force anyone to believe. As Paul says, "So it is with the fear
of the Lord before us that we try to persuade people" (2 Cor.
5:11). Paul says "persuade," not "pester into submission"!

In the past, has anyone been pushy with you, trying to get you to
believe? _____

_____

What persuaded you to believe? _____

_____

The message that we share with others will not always be complete. Sometimes it is necessary to have "pre-evangelistic" conversations. For instance, someone whom we know to be an atheist or
agnostic needs to hear reasons to believe in God's existence.
Sometimes we might see a person regularly and can share with
them a little at a time. But it is vital that in sharing the message of
salvation (the "gospel" or "good news") with others, that we include the "bottom line": Yeshua died for our sins and he rose
from the dead (1 Cor. 15:3–4). "Died for our sins" means that he
already paid the penalty that our sins deserve from God and his
resurrection means that we too can be raised from death.

How does Yeshua's death pay for our sins? _____
_____
_____

Yeshua did not leave us the option of telling others if we felt like doing it. He commanded us to "make *talmidim* [disciples]" (Matt. 28:19). That is, we are to intentionally talk to others about our faith and about the need to turn from sin, believe in Messiah, and start a love relationship with God. Yeshua said, "Likewise, when people light a lamp, they don't cover it with a bowl, but put it on a lampstand so that it shines for everyone in the house" (Matt. 5:15). To not share the message of Yeshua with others is like holding back the light that God gave us to shine out to others.

Have you already had a chance to share the light? Have you had a time yet where you held back from sharing because you were afraid or uncertain how to do so? Explain. _____
_____
_____

Yeshua did not tell us to "make believers" or to "make congregation-attenders," but to make *talmidim*—disciples for him (Matt. 28:19). If someone decides to believe in Yeshua, they need to learn how to follow him. If we do not show them how, or find others who can show them how, then we are leaving them almost as orphans.

What is the difference between someone who is merely a believer and someone who is a disciple? _____
_____
_____
_____

Disciples make other disciples, as Paul says to Timothy: "And these things you heard from me, which were supported by many witnesses, these things commit to faithful people, such as will be competent to teach others also" (2 Tim. 2:2). As you have become a disciple and have learned how to live as a disciple, the task now falls to you to do the same for others.

Homework

Share your testimony with someone else this week. Make a list of people and pray for their salvation. Pray also for opportunities to share the message of Yeshua with them.

Section

DEEPER ISSUES

Three

Introduction

You've learned the basics, the fundamentals of the faith. Now it's time to examine deeper issues for believers. This section does that. It is structured similarly to Section Two, Beginning Steps, and will be helpful in your spiritual growth.

Scripture Study

Key Verse: "The main thing about your word is that it's true; and all your rulings last forever." (Ps. 119:160)

The only way to really learn the Scriptures is to read them—cover to cover. There is no substitute for Bible reading. If you're not already on a Bible reading plan, see below (Bible Reading Plans) and choose a plan that suits your time and ability.

Bible reading should be the mainstay of your spiritual diet. There will be times, however, when you feel a need to study in-depth a particular chapter or paragraph of the Bible. You might do this because you have many questions about the meaning of a particular passage. Or you might do this just for the value of knowing an important chapter of the Bible very deeply. This chapter will teach you principles that will help you study the Scriptures in depth.

Bible Reading Plans

1. Read through the Bible in a year. To do this you will have to read about three and one half chapters per day (there are 1,189 chapters in the Bible).
   a. One way to do this would be to alternate between three chapters on weekdays and four on weekends.
   b. You might read some *Tanakh* (Hebrew Bible or "Old Testament") and some New Testament every day or you might read straight through from Genesis to Revelation.
2. Read the Bible intensively in less than a year. A great way to do this is to read four chapters a day from different parts of the Bible.
   a. If you are using a traditional Jewish Bible, you could simply read one chapter a day in each of these four divisions of the Bible: *Torah*, Prophets, and Writings (found in the Hebrew Bible), and New Testament.

    b. If you are using a traditional Christian Bible, you could read one chapter a day in each of these divisions: Genesis—Esther, Job—Song of Solomon, Isaiah—Malachi, and Matthew—Revelation.

3. Read the Bible at a more leisurely pace.

    a. One chapter a day of Tanakh and New Testament is a good plan.

    b. Alternate between the Tanakh and the New Testament each day, reading only one chapter per day.

The Elements of Bible Study

Good Bible study considers the context, grammar, genre, historical background, and translation of a Bible passage in order to determine a meaning and an application.

Context

Words almost always have more than one meaning. Look in any dictionary and see how few words have only one definition. Context, that which comes before and after a statement, helps us to understand the exact meaning of words and sentences we are studying.

Example: Read Matthew 20:22 by itself without looking at what is said before and after.

What is the cup that Yeshua is about to drink? _____

_____

Now read Matthew 20:17–23.

What is the cup that Yeshua is about to drink? _____

_____

How did the words before verse 22 help to clarify this? _____

_____

There are four kinds of context:
1. Immediate—The words immediately before and after a sentence.
2. Book—The whole of the biblical book you are reading. You can only know from the context of the whole book of Job, for example, to take the words of Job's three "comforters" with a grain of salt.
3. Author—All of the writings of a particular author, such as John or Paul. Paul has a very specific way he uses the term "law" and John has a particular emphasis on "life" that is helpful in understanding any passage in a book they have written.

4. Bible—Sometimes a knowledge of the way a term, such as "the Book of Life," is used throughout the Bible is vital to understand a verse.

Grammar

Since the words of Scripture are God-breathed (2 Tim. 3:16), we must study the words, sentences, and paragraphs God has given us. It is important to remember that God actually gave us his Word in Hebrew, Aramaic, and Greek. The ideal study of the grammar of a passage would be in the original languages. For most people this will not be possible. A second best approach is to look at a minimum of three translations when studying a key verse or phrase (see below—Knowing Your Translations).

Example: Read Romans 8:1.

The word "therefore" at the beginning of this verse is an adverb. Adverbs modify verbs. The verb in this verse is "is awaiting." "Therefore" placed before "there is awaiting" tells the reader that the statement is true because of what came before it. Read Romans 7:24–26. What does the "therefore" refer to in 8:1? _____

_____

_____

Paul is notorious for writing long and complicated sentences. He uses many conjunctions and clauses in his long, complex sentences. One grammatical tool that helps to get the main point of a sentence is to find the main subject, verb, and object of a sentence. Then list the clauses one at a time beneath the main subject, verb, and object. This forms a simple diagram that can make a difficult sentence easier to understand.

Example: Ephesians 1:11, "Also in union with him we were given an inheritance, we who were picked in advance according to the purpose of the One who affects everything in keeping with the decision of his will."

We were given an inheritance . . .
   . . . also
   . . . in union with him
   . . . we who were picked in advance
     . . . according to the purpose of the One
      . . . who affects everything
       . . . in keeping with the decision
        . . . of his will.

Seeing Ephesians 1:11 in this simple diagram, what is the main point of Paul's sentence? _____

_____

_____

Genre

Genre is a fancy word for a type of literature. Genre makes a great difference in how you understand writing. For example, if you are reading a mystery novel, and you hear an in-depth description of a room, then you know that the room's description will probably hold some clue to solving the mystery. On the other hand, if you are reading a real estate advertisement with a detailed description of a house, then you know that you are being given the best possible perspective on a house with the intention of selling it to you. This can make quite a difference in interpreting Scripture.

Example: Read Psalm 19:1 (verse 2 in Jewish Bibles) and then Romans 1:20.

What do both verses have in common? _____

_____

_____

Which verse do you take literally and which verse do you understand poetically? _____

_____

_____

Historical Background

No book of the Bible was written in a historical vacuum. Genesis was written to Israel at the time of the giving of the *Torah* to explain who God is, how the Israelites came from Abraham, and how the Israelites came to be in Egypt. Ruth was written during the time of the Judges, when Israel's disobedience kept bringing curses on them. The book of Ruth was an example of righteousness and blessing to them. Galatians was written to a congregation that was distorting the message of Yeshua into legalism, the idea that keeping certain laws would bring eternal life.

Quite often you can learn historical background from the Bible itself. For example, the book of Ruth begins, "Back in the days when the judges were judging . . ." To learn what those historical times were like, one would need to read the book of Judges. At other times, historical information is best gathered from a Bible Dictionary or a Bible Encyclopedia (see below, A Bible Study Library).

Example: Read Psalm 23:4.

According to a Bible encyclopedia, the rod (*shivat*) is a weapon, which a shepherd would use to kill predators. The staff (*masheynah*) was a walking stick on which the shepherd carried a bag of provisions and which he may have used as a prod to keep the sheep on the path. Knowing this historical background, how would the sheep be comforted by a shepherd's rod and staff? ___

_____

_____

How does the image of the rod and staff refer to God's care for us? _____

_____

Knowing Your Translations

There are two basic kinds of translations: formal equivalent and dynamic equivalent. Formal equivalent translations stay closer to the word order and original phrasing from the Hebrew, Aramaic, or Greek. They are not as readable, however, as dynamic equivalent translations. Dynamic equivalent translations are more loose and more readable. In studying an important verse, it is wise to consult at least three translations, including at least one from each type:

Formal Equivalent	Dynamic Equivalent
King James Version	Complete Jewish Bible
New American Standard Bible	New International Version
Revised Standard Version	Contemporary English Version
New Revised Standard Version	New Living Bible

A Bible Study Library

If and when you are able, you may want to purchase some books to help you study Scripture. These are listed in order of priority; more information for each can be found in the bibliography at the end of this book:

1. A Bible Dictionary or Encyclopedia (suggested: *The New Bible Dictionary* by Tyndale House Publishers or *The International Standard Bible Encyclopedia* by Eerdmans).
2. A Topical Index to the Bible (suggested: *Nave's Topical Bible*).
3. An exhaustive concordance (a book that shows every word used in the Bible and what verses it is used in) in the translation you use.
4. A thorough cross-reference tool (suggested: *The New Treasury of Scripture Knowledge* by Nelson).
5. A book on how to study the Bible (suggested: *How to Read the Bible for All It's Worth* by Gordon Fee and Douglas Stuart).
6. A commentary set to help with difficult passages (suggested: *The Tyndale Old Testament Commentary* and *The Tyndale New Testament Commentaries*).

Homework

Do a study of one or all of the following passages this week, using the material you have learned in this chapter. If you can, borrow a few study books (if you haven't already purchased some). Be able to explain who the characters are, where the places mentioned are, what the point of the passage is, and at what point in history the passage occurs. Also explain any difficult words or sentences in the passage. Write out some study notes, including any questions that you can't answer.

1. Deut. 8:1–10
2. 2 Sam. 7:1–17
3. Ps. 122
4. Rom. 4:1–5

The Bible and Prayer

Key Verse: "Rejoice in your hope, be patient in your troubles, and continue steadfastly in your prayers." (Rom. 12:12)

The biblical example in prayer is powerful. In the lives of men like Moses, David, Elijah, Daniel, Ezra, Nehemiah, Paul, and, of course, Yeshua, prayer is a habit and a means to move God's hand to work on this earth.

Don't look to other believers for an example of what prayer ought to be. Too often, the prayer lives of modern believers are weak and ineffective. Look instead to those in Scripture, whose prayer lives are held up by God as an example for us.

Biblical Occasions for Prayer

In a Crisis: Read 2 Kings 20:1–7.

Does verse 3 seem like a transcript of Hezekiah's entire prayer or just a summary? _____

What effect did Hezekiah's prayer have on God's announced will? How do you know? _____

Requesting Blessings: Read 1 Samuel 1:4–20.

Does verse 11 seem like a transcript of Hannah's prayer or just a summary? _____

What effect did Hannah's prayer have on God's will? How can you tell? _____

For Intimacy With God: Read Exodus 33:7–11.

What seemed to be Moses' purpose in meeting with God? _____

_____

How is Moses' experience the same as our experience in prayer and how is it different? _____

_____

Giving Thanksgiving: Read 1 Chronicles 29:9–13.

What prompted David's thankfulness? _____

Making Confession: Read Psalm 51:1–4 (verses 1–6 in Hebrew Bibles).

Look in the title to this Psalm. What is the occasion of the prayer?

_____

_____

What does David ask for? _____

_____

Praying For Others: Read Acts 12:5–16.

What sort of prayer got Peter out of prison? _____

_____

Yeshua's Prayer Life

Read the following sampling of Yeshua's prayer life and a few of his statements about prayer (he made many more than are listed here). All of these come from just one Gospel.

1. Luke 5:16: "However, he made a practice of withdrawing to remote places to pray."

2. Luke 6:12: "It was around that time that Yeshua went out to the hill country to pray, and all night he continued in prayer to God."

3. Luke 9:28: "About a week after Yeshua said these things, he took Kefa, Yochanan, and Ya'akov [Peter, John, and James] with him and went up into the hill country to pray."

4. Luke 11:1–2: "One time Yeshua was in a certain place praying. As he finished, one of the talmidim [disciples] said to him, 'Sir, teach us to pray, just as Yochanan [John] taught his talmidim."

5. Luke 18:1: "Then Yeshua told his talmidim a parable, in order to impress on them that they must always keep praying and not lose heart."

6. Luke 19:46: "saying to them, 'The Tanakh [Hebrew Bible] says, "My house is to be a house of prayer," but you have made it into a den of robbers.'"

7. Luke 22:32: "But I prayed for you, Shim'on [Simon], that your trust may not fail."

8. Luke 22:40–41: "When he arrived, he said to them, 'Pray that you won't be put to the test.' And he went about a stone's throw away from them, kneeled down and prayed."

9. Luke 22:44–46: "and in great anguish he prayed more intensely, so that his sweat became like drops of blood falling to the ground. On rising from prayer and coming to the talmidim, he found them sleeping because of their grief. He said, 'Why are you sleeping? Get up and pray so that you won't be put to the test!"

From the Scriptures in numbers 1–4 above, what do you learn about Yeshua's habits of prayer? _____

_____

_____

What could you do to develop such habits? _____

_____

What do you learn about some of the content of Yeshua's prayers from number 7? _____

_____

_____

What do you learn about prayer from Yeshua's statements in numbers 5 and 6 and 8? _____

_____

From number 9 we learn one of the greatest lessons of prayer. God is not our "yes-man." Even the godliest person may pray according to God's will and receive a "no." Why did God say "no" to Yeshua? _____

_____

_____

We know that Yeshua never sinned. Yet God did not give him what he asked. Why do you think it was right for Yeshua to ask anyway? _____

_____

The Prayer-book of the Bible

Dietrich Bonhoeffer, the German theologian who died at Flossenburg in a Nazi death camp for conspiring against Hitler, wrote a valuable little volume called Psalms: The Prayer Book of the Bible. In his book, he classifies the Psalms into various kinds or topics of prayer. During the next week, read from and think how you can learn to pray from the Psalms listed below by category:

1. Creation: Ps. 104.
2. *Torah*: Ps. 1 and 19.
3. Holy History: Ps. 78.
4. Messiah: Ps. 110.
5. The Congregation: Ps. 84.
6. Life Needs: Ps. 37.
7. Suffering: Ps. 13.
8. Guilt: Ps. 32.
9. Enemies: Ps. 5.

Homework

Select some verses from at least five of the categories of Psalms above. Use the selected verses as your prayers to God.

Prayer as a Lifestyle

Key Verse: "Pray regularly." (1 Thess. 5:17)

Although the *Complete Jewish Bible* translates 1 Thessalonians 5:17 as "pray regularly," the Greek word (*adialeiptos*) means "without intermission." Prayer for the serious believer is not an occasional activity, but a constant line of communication with God. The only reason the idea of praying without stopping gives people a double-take is that most people limit their concept of prayer to that of dedicated time, away from others and with their bodies in a certain position. Without kneeling and folding of hands, many people would say prayer has not occurred.

But prayer is more than a bodily position, solitude, and certain formulas of words. Prayer is conversation and communion (even silent communion) with God. Sometimes this may involve getting alone, kneeling, prostrating, raising hands, or other features. Most often, for those who understand prayer, this communion will happen with busyness all around us. There will be no special position, nor will we be alone, nor will words be spoken out loud, and sometimes no words will be spoken even in our minds. We will just know we are with him, and that is enough.

The Everything, All-the-Time Commands

1. "Well, whatever you do, whether it's eating or drinking or anything else, do it all so as to bring glory to God" (1 Cor. 10:31).
2. "Always give thanks for everything to God the Father in the name of our Lord Yeshua the Messiah" (Eph. 5:20).
3. "Don't worry about anything; on the contrary, make your requests known to God by prayer and petition, with thanksgiving" (Phil. 4:6).
4. "That is, everything you do or say, do in the name of the Lord Yeshua, giving thanks through him to God the Father" (Col. 3:17).
5. "We always thank God for you, regularly mentioning you in our prayers" (1 Thess. 1:2).
6. "Always be joyful. Pray regularly. In everything give thanks, for this is what God wants from you who are united in Messiah" (1 Thess. 5:16–18).

When should we thank God? _____

_____

When should we praise him? _____

_____

How often should we be in conversation with him? _____

_____

Why don't we do this? _____

_____

Practicing God's Presence

Sometimes the strangest figures can teach us great lessons. Imagine learning about prayer from a dishwasher in a monastery in France during the 1600s. Nicholas Herman was just such a man. He is better known as Brother Lawrence. He presented so clearly what God is saying to us in these commands to pray always.

In the drudgery of washing dishes for hundreds of monks, Brother Lawrence became known for always being in conversation with God. In his letters, in a sparse number of brief writings, and in some interviews held with him, the blessing that he found was passed on to us in a little book called *The Practice of the Presence of God*. Here is a sampling of what he has to say:

> "Brother Lawrence insisted that it is necessary to always be aware of God's presence by talking with him throughout each day. To think that you must abandon conversation with him in order to deal with the world is erroneous."—From the First Conversation
>
> "He believed it was a serious mistake to think of our prayer time as being different from any other. Our actions should unite us with God when we are involved in our daily activities, just as our prayer unites us with him in our quiet time."—Fourth Conversation
>
> "He said his prayers consisted totally and simply of God's presence. His soul was resting in God, having lost its awareness of everything but him. When he wasn't in

prayer, he felt practically the same way. Remaining near to God, he praised him and blessed him with all his strength. Because of this, his life was full of continual joy."—Fourth Conversation

"The most holy and necessary practice in our spiritual life is the presence of God. That means finding constant pleasure in his divine company, speaking humbly and lovingly with him at all seasons, at every moment, without limiting the conversation in any way. This is especially important in times of temptation, sorrow, separation from God, and even in times of unfaithfulness and sin."—From Spiritual Maxims

There are times of concentrated prayer, where we are in solitude and focused on no other activity but talking with God. There are times of corporate prayer, where we are in a group of believers praying together. The majority of the time in our lives, however, will be spent in other activities. Right now, how frequently do you speak with God in your mind during these times? _____

How does the prayer style practiced by Brother Lawrence fit "the everything, all-the-time" commands? _____

Prayer-styles, Jewishness, and God's Leading

There are very different styles of prayer that people choose. In Judaism, the use of the *siddur*, the Jewish prayer book, for *shacharit*, *minchah*, and *ma'ariv* (morning, afternoon, and evening prayers) is the traditional standard. For some Messianic Jewish believers, this traditional Jewish method will be appealing (see the upcoming chapter on the *siddur*, in Section Five). Others will find it time-consuming and unfulfilling. Each person must allow God to guide in issues of prayer style.

Other issues in prayer style involve choosing between a morning time, mid-day, or evening for a period of concentrated prayer. Some people pray in the morning and others in the evening, and there are Scripture references for all of them. Daniel prayed three times a day, which is still the pattern for traditional Jewish observance. Various Scriptures speak of prayer in the morning and at night (Ps. 5:3; 55:17; 88:1, 13; 143:8; and Isa. 33:2).

A well-balanced prayer life should include some concentrated prayer (including praise, thanksgiving, confession, petition, and intercession), corporate prayer, and practicing God's presence throughout our daily activities. Real closeness with God happens in the prayer closet, in the prayer circle, and in the awareness of God's presence throughout the activities of the day.

What prayer times and styles have you tried? _____

_____

What prayer times and styles would you like to try now? _____

_____

Homework

Following are some prayer methods for you to experiment with. There are numerous methods, styles, and subjects of prayer. To learn more about the variety of prayer traditions, read Richard Foster's *Prayer: Finding the Heart's True Home* (see bibliography). Try at least one of these prayer exercises throughout the week this week.

1. Try praying the daily prayers from the *siddur*. Use the Hebrew only if you understand it. Pray the prayers in English if you don't understand the Hebrew. If you are unfamiliar with the prayers in the *siddur*, it may help to read the chapter below, "Praying the *Siddur*."
2. Make a prayer list, which you may keep regularly updated. Every time you think of some need to pray about or some aspect of God to praise him for, add it to your list. Set aside time regularly, either daily or weekly, to pray through your list.
3. Going one step further than a prayer list, keep a prayer journal. Include not only requests and praises, but also any answers you see to your prayers, including dates.
4. Prayer walking is simply talking to God as you walk through an area. Generally a prayer walk is undertaken as a way to pray

for a neighborhood, a congregation, a school, or some other community or organization. You might walk through the neighborhood where friends and family live and pray for them. Perhaps there is a Jewish neighborhood near you where you can pray for your Jewish people to come to know Messiah. Sometimes, walking while praying is a good idea just to help you concentrate, even if you are not especially praying for the neighborhood through which you are walking.

5. Find a group through your congregation that meets to pray and join them. If there is no such group, perhaps you can form one. Just bringing together a group for one meeting is worthwhile, even if you are not planning on meeting regularly.

6. Write down some Scripture references, such as in the Psalms, that make good prayers. There are numerous prayers in the Bible that you can use (e.g. Exod. 15:2–3, 11–13; Ps. 8; Eph. 1:15–21; Rev. 4:11). Try using them in your prayer time.

7. Try practicing God's presence all through the day. Notice what activities and what times of the day tend to make you forget about God's presence. Make an effort to think of him every minute. Most people find this difficult and a lot of practice is required. If you keep it up, you'll think of him and speak to him more and more often.

The Ins and Outs of Congregations

Key Verse: "The leaders who lead well should be considered worthy of double honor, especially those working hard at communicating the word and teaching." (1 Tim. 5:17)

Leadership is so essential to the working of a congregation that the Apostles never failed to appoint leaders in the works that they planted. Luke writes of Paul and his companions in their journeys to make disciples:

> After proclaiming the Good News in that city and making many people into *talmidim*, they returned to Lystra, Iconium, and Antioch, strengthening the *talmidim*, encouraging them to remain true to the faith, and reminding them that it is through many hardships that we must enter the kingdom of God. After appointing elders for them in every congregation, Sha'ul and Bar-Nabba [Paul and Barnabas], with prayer and fasting, committed them to the Lord in whom they had put their trust. (Acts 14:21–23)

Even though the people in these places had known the Lord only a short time, the apostles deemed it necessary to appoint leaders among them.

Most congregations, Messianic Jewish or otherwise, have one visible leader who does most of the teaching. It is common for other leaders over areas of the congregation to be appointed as well. Some of these will be vocational (paid) and others volunteer. The workings of a congregation and the leadership of a congregation are laid out in Scripture so that all believers can work together, under leadership, to fulfill God's plan.

Teaching

One of the important functions of a congregation is the teaching of the Scriptures, of life in Messiah, and of important truths (doctrine) about God and his ways. In the New Testament, the person leading the congregational teaching is referred to variously as an "elder" (Gk. *presbyteros*), "overseer" (Gk. *episcope*), and a "shepherd" (Gk. *poimen*). These three titles for the congregational leaders are interchangeable:

> Therefore, I urge the congregational leaders [*presbyteros*] among you, as a fellow leader and witness of Messiah's sufferings, as well as a sharer in the glory to be revealed: shepherd [*poimaino*] the flock of God that is in your care . . . (1 Pet. 5:1–2)
>
> Furthermore, he gave some people as emissaries, some as prophets, some as proclaimers of the Good News, and some as shepherds and teachers. (Eph. 4:12)

Differing titles such as rabbi, pastor, leader, or elder are common. Though some congregations have more than one such leader, in most cases one leader is in charge and other leaders are under him to guide, direct, and shepherd the congregation.

The teaching task in the congregation is carried out under the direction of the leader of the congregation who is responsible to God for the spiritual health of the congregation (Heb. 3:17). The concept of a teacher as the highest office in the congregation is nothing new to those raised in Judaism. Rabbis, like the congregational leaders of the New Testament, are generally those with extra training and experience to lead groups spiritually.

The three biblical terms for the congregational leader are instructive:

1. Elder (*presbyteros*) speaks of experience as a factor in the selection of leaders. Age is not always the primary factor (1 Tim. 4:12), but experience in walking in the lifestyle of Messiah is important.
2. Overseer (*episcope*) may be related to the president or *nasi* of the ancient synagogue. This role overlaps with and yet is distinct from the role of an elder. An overseer directs the congregation in business matters. Often, the overseer and elder roles are combined into one person, although the synagogue pattern was to separate them between the rabbi and the *nasi*.
3. Shepherd (*poimen*) speaks of guidance and care for spiritual needs.

A congregational leader is responsible for the teaching, directing, and tending of souls.

How do you see the aspects of elder/overseer/shepherd in your congregational leader? _____

_____

What other leaders are you aware of in your congregation besides the main leader? _____

_____

_____

Worship

For most people, worship equals music about God. Actually, worship is a bigger concept than religious music. Worship refers to the giving of something of ourselves back to God. We might give our adoration, either in song or in non-musical prayer. We might give our money, in congregational and mission offerings. We might give of our labor or time. All of these are worship.

Musical worship is vital to the faith handed down to us by the patriarchs, prophets, and apostles. Moses used musical worship (Exod. 15). Later in Israelite history, the Levitical families were organized into choirs and orchestras, playing music during the Tabernacle ceremonies (1 Chron. 15:22; 25:7; 2 Chron. 29:27). In modern Judaism, the cantor (*chazzan*) serves as the primary worship leader.

Music leaders and musicians are still a big part of congregational life. The New Testament speaks of believers sharing music with one another, "sing psalms, hymns, and spiritual songs to each other; sing to the Lord and make music in your heart to him" (Eph. 5:19). The congregational leader generally leads worship in other areas, such as the teaching of the Scriptures, the Lord's Supper, and immersion.

Who are the worship leaders that you are aware of in your congregation? _____

_____

Service

The Body of Messiah is called to serve two groups of people: others in the body and those outside of the congregation who need to know Messiah's love. In particular, there is a need to serve those who are less able to help themselves: widows, single mothers, the elderly, and orphans or children from broken homes (James 1:27).

In the early congregation in Jerusalem, there arose a need for leaders in areas of service to be appointed. The specific problem at the time involved providing food for widows. The congregational leaders were too busy to work in all of the areas of service and maintain their role as teachers and shepherds. Men were appointed as servants (deacons or ministers) to lead in areas of service (Acts 6:1–6). Paul taught that such men and women, leading in areas of service, should meet certain qualifications, including integrity and faith (1 Tim. 3:8–13). In some congregations, the deacons serve more as leaders assisting the pastor (like a governing board). Regardless of the title used in your congregation, there are those men and women who lead in areas of service.

Who are the leaders in areas of service that you are aware on in your congregation? _____

_____

Evangelism

Another important area of responsibility in the body of Messiah is evangelism—the propagation of the faith. Congregational leaders are almost always involved in the job of telling others about Messiah. Other leaders, called evangelists, or missionaries, especially work in the area of getting the good news of repentance, faith, and a relationship with God through Yeshua to those who have not yet embraced the faith. Ultimately, all believers are evangelists with a small "e" and some are especially gifted by God as Evangelists with a big "E."

Evangelists may work through a local congregation, leading in various outreaches of the congregation. At other times, evangelists are sent out to other places, sometimes far away, to spread the good news.

Who are some leaders in evangelism at your congregation or out on the field supported by your congregation? _____

_____

Administration

Although it may look easy, you can bet that a great deal of work goes on behind the scenes running your congregation. Moneys are collected, deposited, and accounted for thoroughly. Materials are ordered and kept on hand. Bills are paid and facilities maintained. Volunteers and employees are coordinated. A lot of work that seems "non-spiritual" goes on at a congregation.

One of the spiritual gifts that God blesses the congregation with is service (Rom. 12:7). The leaders in service at the congregation could be seen as operating in two areas—service to those in need and service in running the congregation. We already spoke about the first kind of service. But the second is equally important. God has blessed the congregation with people who like to serve behind the scenes. Without their gifting and work, very little would get done in God's kingdom.

Who are the leaders and servers in the administration of your congregation? _____

_____

Putting it All Together

The congregation is designed by God to be both a community and an organism. As a community we gather and are a part of one another's lives. As an organism, we function according to certain principles, while not becoming a bureaucracy of separate entities. That is, people in the community come together to lead or help in the areas which God has appointed as necessary for the functioning of the congregation. In the areas of teaching, worship, service, evangelism, and administration, there are helpers and leaders.

But the various parts of the body are not separate. God teaches us that we are a body whose individual parts are interrelated and interdependent (1 Cor. 12). As you begin to see how your congregation works, you will not want to sit on the sidelines. You will be led by God to get involved. Perhaps at first you will be a helper in one area. As you learn and grow you may become a helper or a leader in other areas. To be healthy in your relationship with God, it is vital that you become involved.

Homework

Meet with your congregational leader or with another leader in your congregation to discuss your involvement in helping.

Finances and the Believer

Key Verse: "Moreover, God has the power to provide you with every gracious gift in abundance, so that always, in every way, you will have all you need yourselves and be able to provide abundantly for every good cause." (2 Cor. 9:9)

Becoming a believer in Yeshua will bring some changes to your financial life. The Scriptures have a great deal to say on the subject of finances. God cares about your resources and has given principles dealing with supporting kingdom work, keeping debts to a minimum, and being generous to others within the body and outside of it who are in need.

Misquoted probably more than any other verse in the Bible, 1 Timothy 6:10 is usually rendered, "Money is the root of all evil." Well, Paul actually said, "For the love of money is a root of all the evils; because of this craving, some people have wandered away from the faith and pierced themselves to the heart with many pains." Money is not a bad thing. With great amounts of donated money the Tabernacle (and later, the Temple) were built (Exod. 25). The problem is not money itself, but the great desire for money causes people to do evil things. Following Yeshua, however, means deciding between money and Yeshua as master of our lives, "No one can be slave to two masters; for he will either hate the first and love the second, or scorn the second and be loyal to the first. You can't be a slave to both God and money" (Matt. 6:24).

Supporting Kingdom Work

The first thing you must know about giving your money to support God's work is that God doesn't need it. "If I were hungry I would not tell you," God says, "for the world is mine and everything in it" (Ps. 50:12). It is not your money that God wants, but your heart. If you are not willing to give generously and sacrificially to God's work, then he does not have your heart. Any cause that does not affect a person's wallet is not a cause he or she is really committed to.

You will frequently hear people talking about a "tithe." The tithe is a ten percent share of money and goods. Many people do not really know how the tithes were used in Israel. The key Scriptures regarding the laws of the tithe are:

> "Every year you must take one tenth of everything your seed produces in the field and eat it in the presence of *ADONAI* your God" (Deut. 14:22).
>
> "At the end of every three years you are to take all the tenths of your produce from that year and store it in your towns. Then the Levi [Levite], because he has no share or inheritance like yours, along with the foreigner, the orphan, and the widow living in your towns, will come, eat, and be satisfied—so that *ADONAI* your God will bless you in everything that you do" (Deut. 14:28–29).

See also Num. 18:21–26; Deut. 12:17; 26:12.

The principle of the tithe was twofold:

1. It served as a great feast every two out of three years at the Tabernacle (later the Temple) for all to share in.
2. It was an offering every third year to the Levites and those who would have difficulty making a living.

The tithe law cannot be literally applied today, since we no longer have a Temple system or a tribal system. Most believers today assume that the tithe law means giving ten percent of our earnings every week in congregation. The truth is, that is not a biblical commandment. For if we did do that according to the tithe laws, we should use the proceeds two out of three years for a great feast!

Rather than seeing the tithe laws as a straightforward commandment to bring ten percent of our resources in to the congregation every week, we should see it as a well chosen divine number to guide us into how much giving to aim for. In other words, while we cannot follow the tithe laws literally, we can consider them a guideline for giving. The principle of the tithe law is that we must support the work of the kingdom, which means God's work in the world, and that we must provide for those who have trouble providing for themselves. Ten percent of our resources is a good number to go by.

How do you feel about setting aside ten percent of your income as a way to support the work of the kingdom? _____

_____

Another biblical principle of giving is called firstfruits. According to Exodus 34:36, "You are to bring the best firstfruits of your land into the house of ADONAI your God." The principle is two-fold:

1. You are first to give to God from your income and keep what comes after to use as he directs you.
2. You are to give God the best portion, not just the things that you can't use.

Oftentimes, when people give old clothing or toys to a charity, they give things that are no longer useful. It is good to take things we can no longer use and give them to others who can. But God is not a charity. We don't give him castoffs, but ought to give him the best of our income, our time, and most of all, our love. In terms of financial giving, this means that our giving should cost us something. Some people have so much money that giving ten percent will not even dent their lifestyle. Our giving ought to cost us if it is really a sacrifice.

Another concept in biblical giving is the freewill offering. Numerous Scriptures refer to a freewill offering, such as Deuteronomy 16:10, "You are to observe the festival of *Shavu'ot* [Weeks, also called Pentecost] for ADONAI your God with a voluntary offering, which you are to give in accordance with the degree to which ADONAI your God has prospered you." Freewill offerings are collected today for special needs, for missionaries, and for other special ministries. In the first century, a special freewill offering was collected for the poor in the Jerusalem congregation. Paul traveled and collected money for this offering and gave this additional principle for the freewill giving, "Each should give according to what he has decided in his heart, not grudgingly or under compulsion, for God loves a cheerful giver" (2 Cor. 9:7).

Giving to support God's kingdom is a major topic in Scripture, covered in numerous passages of the Bible with examples, principles, and commandments. Here is a summary of the principles given above:

1. Set aside the first and the best of your resources for God's work in the congregation and in other ministries.
2. Support the work of the congregational leaders as a first priority, just as Levites and Priests were a first priority in the tithe law.
3. Help those who are in positions that make it difficult to earn a living, such as single moms, the elderly, handicapped people, etc.
4. Set aside a regular amount, with ten percent being a good guideline, for your regular, weekly giving.
5. Look for opportunities to give freewill offerings above and beyond your regular giving.
6. Give to God's work in proportion to the way God has blessed you. In other words, a percentage system for giving makes good sense.
7. Give deliberately and cheerfully, not resenting God for commanding you to support his work.
8. God doesn't need our money; he demands our hearts' devotion and he comes before all our other needs.

Which of these principles of giving have you been practicing and which ones do you need to begin practicing? _____

_____

_____

_____

Keeping Debts to a Minimum and Guarding Your Flocks

God cares about our financial well-being. He cares because he wants to bless us, and will bless us if we live according to his commandments (2 Cor. 9:6–11). Part of God's plan is that we will not allow our resources to be squandered on debt or foolish neglect. Solomon exhorts us to take good care of our finances:

> Take care to know the condition of your flocks, and pay attention to your herds.
> For wealth doesn't last forever, neither does a crown through all generations.
> When the hay has been mown, and the new grass appears, and the mountain greens have been gathered; the lambs

will provide your clothing, the goats will sell for enough to buy a field, and there will be enough goat's milk to [buy] food for you and your household and maintenance for your servant-girls. (Prov. 27:23–27)

Taking care of our finances is important so that: (1) we will be able to provide for ourselves in old age, (2) we will be able to support God's work, and (3) we will not unnecessarily become a burden on others.

Perhaps the two most important biblical principles for financial well-being are diligence and freedom from debt. Regarding diligence, the Proverbs have much to say:

Idle hands bring poverty; diligent hands bring wealth.
The diligent will rule, while the lazy will be put to forced labor.
The lazy person wants but doesn't have; the diligent get their desires fulfilled.
In all work there is profit, but mere talk produces only poverty.
If you love sleep you will become poor; keep your eyes open, and you'll have plenty of food.
(Prov. 10:4; 12:24; 13:4; 14:23; 20:13)

Regarding freedom from debts, the Proverbs again gives us wisdom, "The rich rule the poor and the borrower is slave to the lender" (Prov. 22:7). Laziness and debt will ruin us.

Paul says, "Don't owe anyone anything—except to love one another" (Rom. 13:8). It is not wise to get into a position of owing money to others, for this gives us benefits today at the cost of tomorrow's resources. What we should be doing is just the opposite, saving some of today's resources for tomorrow's benefit. And laziness is the ultimate in squandering our potential. Hard work will enable us to provide for ourselves, for others, and for God's work.

What areas of your financial life need work? _____

_____

Homework

If you do not have one, make a budget for your monthly and weekly expenses and income. Plan your regular giving prayerfully. Consider ways to set aside money for special needs and freewill offerings. If you have debt, make plans to pay it off as fast as you can and as slowly as you need to.

Holy Living

Key Verse: "Keep pursuing *shalom* with everyone and the holiness without which no one will see the Lord." (Heb. 12:14)

Sooner or later, the Holy Spirit creates a desire in the heart of every believer to go beyond the old life and to more fully move into the new life. Many believers in Yeshua are content for a while to keep moving in the same patterns of sin that characterized life before Yeshua. But a growing discontentment gnaws at most: discontentment with the pleasures of sin, and a longing for a higher life.

This desire for righteousness is given by the Holy Spirit and is the chief purpose of his work in our lives. Yeshua said, "How blessed are those who hunger and thirst for righteousness! For they will be filled" (Matt. 6:6). That hungering and thirsting is the desire that the Holy Spirit gives.

Perhaps you feel it when you are around others further along in the faith than yourself. Maybe it is in reading about God and his holiness. Maybe it is in contemplating the Lord's Supper and the meaning of the death of Yeshua. You probably feel this desire and God has not left you as an orphan to figure out on your own how to live a holy life. He will guide you and provide you with everything you need.

What Holiness Is and What God Expects

Holiness is a separation from sinful deeds and thoughts and a separation unto God. In other words, it is turning away from sinful patterns and toward Godly patterns of living, thinking, and feeling.

God taught Israel about the importance of holiness throughout the *Torah*. Using tangible regulations regarding diet, maintaining a pure Tabernacle/Temple, and being a people separate from evil and uncleanness, God demonstrated in numerous ways in the *Torah* his aversion to sin:

> "In this way, you will separate the people of Israel from their uncleanness, so that they will not die in a state

of uncleanness for defiling my Tabernacle which is among them" (Lev. 15:31).

"Anyone who touches something unclean—whether the uncleanness be from a person, from an unclean animal or from some other unclean detestable thing—and then eats from the meat from the sacrifice of peace offerings, that person will be cut off from his people" (Lev. 7:21).

"You will distinguish between the holy and the common, and between the unclean and the clean" (Lev. 10:10).

"You are not to engage in the activities found in the land of Egypt, where you used to live; and you are not to engage the activities found in the land of Kena'an [Canaan], where I am bringing you; nor are you to live by their laws" (Lev. 18:3).

Some of the things which God called unclean in the *Torah* are not acts of sin, such as touching a dead person. It is not wrong to touch a dead person and sometimes this is required, such as when one of our loved ones dies. These issues were not called sins or transgressions, but uncleanness. God set up the clean and unclean laws as a physical picture of a spiritual reality.

The rules of clean and unclean were elaborate and involved keeping the Tabernacle and the altar pure from a list of contaminants. The spiritual reality behind all of this is the absolute holiness of God, his total aversion to sin, and the incompatibility of even minor sin with God's presence. Were it not for the cleansing that we receive through Yeshua's death, according to the laws of blood sacrifice, we would not be able to stand in God's presence.

The fact that we have been granted a cleansing is often called *positional holiness.* But God wants more than just positional holiness; he wants us to move on to *practical holiness.* Practical holiness is a separation from sinful thoughts and deeds.

From what you know about the laws of cleanness and uncleanness in the Torah, can you see the lesson God was teaching? Explain.

_____

_____

_____

God told Israel in Leviticus 18:3 to avoid the ways of the Egyptians and the Canaanites. What parallels would you make to the ways of people in our godless society? _____

_____

_____

Who Makes Us Holy?

There is a basic tension between two sides in the holiness equation. On the one hand, holiness is something God builds into our lives:

> ". . . and we are being changed into his very image, from one degree of glory to the next, by *ADONAI* the Spirit." (2 Cor. 3:18)

According to Paul, in this verse, we are being made more like Yeshua, a little at a time by the work of God in our lives. On the other hand, we are to discipline ourselves and pursue holiness:

> "Now every athlete in training submits himself to strict discipline, and he does it to win a laurel wreath that will soon wither away. But we do it to win a crown that will last forever." (1 Cor. 9:25)

Here Paul speaks of our growth in holiness like an athlete's training. It involves discipline and consistent work. The seasoned athlete may make his or her performance look easy, but you can bet a great deal of work lay behind it.

How can both sides be true? How can God work in us to make us holy and yet we are also to work to make ourselves holy? This is not merely an example of the old adage, "God helps those who help themselves." Rather, God does his part in the work of making us holy and we do our part. If we fail to do our part, God keeps working, but on a broken-down machine, as it were. If we cooperate with God in the work, then the process goes along much faster. The more we fail to cooperate, oftentimes the more drastic measures God will use—including physical harm, stress, illness, or bereavement. Paul sums up the full picture of our part and

God's part when he says: ". . . keep working out your deliverance [from sin] with fear and trembling, for God is the one working among you both the willing and the working for what pleases him" (Phil. 2:12–13).

What is your understanding of the source of holiness is your life?

_____

_____

How To Grow in Holiness

There are numerous teachings in the Bible about ways to grow in holiness. There are numerous avenues and methods that will help. Paul especially has a lot to say about practical holiness, but really there is help throughout the Bible. As followers of Yeshua, endowed with the Holy Spirit, we have resources for holiness that were not available to believers who lived before Yeshua. One overarching principle of life in Yeshua goes before all others as an encouragement to holiness:

"God's power has given us everything we need for life and godliness, through our knowing the One who called us to his own glory and goodness." (2 Pet. 1:3)

"No temptation has seized you beyond what people normally experience, and God can be trusted not to allow you to be tempted beyond what you can bear. On the contrary, along with the temptation he will also provide a way out, so that you will be able to endure." (1 Cor. 10:13)

The principle is: *we do not have to sin, God has given us the ability to say 'no.'* Certain understandings and certain practices will make the job of living holy lives easier. Below is a sample of scriptural principles designed to help us in this.

1. Do it out of love for God: "Therefore, you are to love *ADONAI* your God and always obey his commission, regulations, rulings, and *mitzvot* [commandments]" (Deut. 11:1). "You are my friends, if you do what I command you" (John 15:14).

2. Learn and even memorize God's teachings, especially the commandments: "Therefore you are to store up these words of mine in your heart and in all your being; tie them on your hand as a sign; put them at the front of a headband around your forehead" (Deut. 11:18).

3. Don't be discouraged; his commandments are not too hard: "For this *mitzvah* I am giving you today is not too hard for you, it is not beyond your reach" (Deut. 30:11).

4. Believe that God can give you strength to obey: "For loving God means obeying his commandments. Moreover, his commandments are not burdensome, because everything that has God as its Father overcomes the world. And this is what victoriously overcomes the world: our trust" (1 John 5:3–4).

5. Put your emphasis first on the greater issues of holiness (don't major on the minors): "Human being, you have already been told what is good, what *ADONAI* demands of you—no more than to act justly, love grace and walk in purity with your God" (Mic. 6:8). "Woe to you hypocritical *Torah*-teachers and *P'rushim* [Pharisees]! You pay your tithes of mint, dill, and cumin; but you have neglected the weightier matters of the *Torah*—justice, mercy, trust. These are the things you should have attended to—without neglecting the others!" (Matt. 23:23)

6. Make it a practice to keep your thoughts and desires in the realm of good and godly things. The real battle is in your mind: "For those who identify with the old nature [our old sinful ways] set their minds on the things of the old nature, but those who identify with the Spirit set their minds on things of the Spirit" (Rom. 8:5). "Focus your minds on things above, not on things here on earth" (Col. 3:2).

7. By the regular practice of thinking godly thoughts, allow your mind to be transformed into holiness: "In other words, do not let yourselves be conformed to the standards of the *'olam hazeh* [this world]. Instead, keep letting yourselves be transformed by the renewing of your minds . . ." (Rom. 12:2)

8. Be disciplined about spiritual exercises, especially prayer and Scripture meditation or reading (but also including such things as fasting, solitude, memorizing Scripture, practicing God's presence, worshipping with a congregation or groups

of believers, and meeting with other believers to discuss sin issues): "Now every athlete in training submits himself to strict discipline, and he does it to win a laurel wreath that will soon wither away. But we do it to win a crown that will last forever" (1 Cor. 9:25).

What principles from this list have you already been using? _____

_____

_____

Are there any principles that you would add to this list? If so, what? _____

_____

Homework

Using the principles on the list above, spend some time working on holiness in your life. Write about the results to share them with someone this week.

Spiritual Gifts

Key Verse: "Moreover, to each person is given the particular manifestation of the Spirit that will be for the common good." (1 Cor. 12:7)

The congregation is like a body. Every member has a part in the function of the body. The body is unhealthy when any member will not perform its function. Some parts are more vital than others. The body can survive if one hand quits functioning, although it will be impaired. When a kidney shuts down things become serious. If the heart quits, then the body dies.

It seems that few congregations have a fully functioning and healthy body. Most are missing fingers and toes, because many people are not picking up their place and function in the body. What is it that God is calling you to do in the congregation? To answer this question, we must examine the special gifts that God has given to the members of the body. These spiritual gifts are special abilities that meet needs in the congregation.

Paul's Instructions on Spiritual Gifts

There are three passages in the Bible that deal with the issue of spiritual gifts. It is only from looking at all three of them that we can get a complete look at the roles God has assigned in the congregation.

"But we have gifts that differ and which are meant to be used according to the grace which has been given to us. If your gift is prophecy, use it to the extent of your trust; if it is serving, use it to serve; if you are a teacher, use your gift in teaching; if you are a counselor, use your gift to comfort and exhort; if you are someone who gives, do it simply and generously; if you are in a position of leadership, lead with diligence and zeal; if you are one who does acts of mercy, do them cheerfully." (Rom. 12:6–8)

"Now there are different kinds of gifts, but the same Spirit gives them. Also there are different ways of serving, but it is the same Lord being served. And there are different modes of working, but it is the same God working them all in everyone. Moreover, to each person is given the particular manifestation of the Spirit that will be for the common good. To one, through the Spirit, is given a word of wisdom; to another, a word of knowledge, in accordance with the same Spirit; to another, faith, by the same Spirit; and to another, healing, by the one Spirit; to another, the working of miracles; to another, prophecy; to another, the ability to judge between spirits; to another, the ability to speak in different kinds of tongues; and to yet another, the ability to interpret tongues." (1 Cor. 12:4–10)

"Furthermore, he gave some people as emissaries, some as prophets, some as proclaimers of the Good News, and some as shepherds and teachers." (Eph. 4:12)

General Principles About Spiritual Gifts

Before looking at the gifts individually, it is important to understand some general principles from these Scriptures:

1. "We have gifts that differ"—Too often a person feels that everyone else ought to feel burdened in the same areas of congregational service that they are involved in. "Why doesn't everybody want to teach the youth? Don't they know the youth are the future of the congregation?" But Paul teaches us that not all have the same gifts and callings.
2. ". . . meant to be used according to the grace given us."—We must use the gifts. Otherwise, God has blessed us and we are refusing his gift. We must use them to the extent that God has given us the ability to use them. A teacher just starting out should not try to match the work of a seasoned teacher, but neither should a seasoned teacher settle for the same basic lessons and techniques of a beginner. The gifts should be used according to the amount of ability God has given.
3. ". . . the same Spirit gives them."—Evangelists shouldn't look down on teachers or servers. Nor should servers think more highly or lowly of teachers and leaders. The Spirit knows what

87

he is doing when he gives gifts. If a person is serving according to his or her calling, whether it seems like a higher calling or a lower one, obedience is taking place.

4. ". . . the same Lord being served."—We are not serving the congregation, but ultimately we are serving God. This will affect how you look at your role. There are often reasons why we can doubt that the congregation is worth our efforts, but there is no doubt God is worth our very best.

5. "Moreover to each person is given the particular manifestation of the Spirit . . ."—Everyone has a spiritual gift, even new believers. No one has a reason to stay out of a role of service in the congregation.

6. ". . . that will be for the common good."—The spiritual gifts are not for us to enjoy or boast about, but for the good of the whole congregation. Nor can we sit by and be spectators. We might feel that it is our personal business, but by not using the gifts God has given, we are stealing from the congregation.

How are you serving right now? How do you think you could be serving? _____

_____

_____

_____

The Gifts Explained

1. Prophecy—This gift refers to speaking God's words, just like the biblical prophets. Some people see this as a miraculous gift, as in the biblical prophets, and others see it as one who can see errors and point them out. Based upon the accounts of prophets in the book of Acts, it seems best to see this as a miraculous gift—being given words from God directly to give to the people. To claim to speak prophetically when the words are your own is a great sin, punishable by death in the days of the *Torah* (Deut. 18).

2. Serving—Quite simply, this gift involves helping others. This may mean help in the congregation or outside of it. The Greek word is the same word from which we get the title of "deacon."

3. Teaching—There are many different kinds of teaching. Some are gifted at speaking to large groups, others at leading de-

tailed studies, others with small groups, some with children, some with adults, and the variations are many.

4. Counseling—Exhortation, warning, holding people accountable, encouraging, and advising are all a part of this gift. Counselors like to work with people and their problems.

5. Giving—Some people love to find ways to give money or other resources to support God's work. These people feel especially burdened to meet the needs of God's servants and of those who come into various crises.

6. Leading/Shepherding—Presiding over meetings and helping people successfully do the work of ministry is the gift of leadership. Leaders like to empower other people, not do it all themselves. Leaders are comfortable holding people to standards and enabling them to grow.

7. Acts of Mercy—Some people are especially burdened to help those in mourning and suffering. Visiting the sick and prisoners, comforting the bereaved, and helping the needy are all examples of this gift.

8. Wisdom—Some see this gift as similar to what Solomon was given, which enabled him to write Proverbs and Ecclesiastes. This is the gift of being able to apply knowledge to life and to help others see the wise course of action. Others see this as a prophetic gift of being able to speak out wisdom directly from God (since the text uses the expression "word of wisdom").

9. Knowledge—In similar fashion to wisdom, some see this as a gift of intellect and some see it as a miraculous gift. As an intellectual gift, this could refer to those with knowledge of history, theology, Scripture, and other useful disciplines that can sharpen the body. If the gift, called a "word of knowledge," is like a prophetic gift, then it may refer to being given knowledge of a specific situation that only God could know. For example, someone might rebuke you for a sin that only God could know you committed.

10. Faith—Those with the gift of faith are an inspiration to others and strengthen them when times are hard. People with this gift are a pleasure to be around when you have been depressed or are facing difficulties ahead. Their unwavering trust in the goodness of God will heal fear and doubt.

11. Healing—Most people agree that this is a miraculous gift, although it may also apply to the work of physicians and

surgeons. Biblical healing was not done to bring glory to anyone but God. Biblical healings were also dramatic (e.g. withered hands restored, blind and deaf restored to sight and sound, etc.).

12. Miracles—It is difficult to know what other sorts of miracles, besides healing or prophecy, this could refer to. Yeshua did miracles beyond healings, such as calming storms. Perhaps God has gifted or will gift some to perform signs and wonders of great magnitude like Yeshua did.

13. Judging Spirits—Many people assume that any believer can deal with demonic possession and issues of the spirit world. However, this Scripture, as well as Yeshua's words to his disciples, suggest that ability to cast out or speak to demons could be a spiritual gift given to certain people. This gift is taken by some in a non-miraculous sense of people being able to detect subtle errors in teaching.

14. Tongues/Languages—Much confusion exists about this gift. In Greek, as well as in Hebrew, "tongues" means "languages." All agree that this gift refers to supernatural ability to speak languages unknown by the speaker (e.g. a missionary miraculously able to speak to Chinese people in their language without training). Some also feel this gift refers to heavenly languages, or angelic ones, that are unknown to man. This gift is believed by all to be used at times in evangelism to speakers of a foreign language. Some also believe in a "prayer language," a special heavenly language. Praying in this special language, in words that the one praying cannot understand, is a way of praying beyond the intellect. Although some people insist that this one gift should belong to all believers, Paul specifically says it is given to some, not all (1 Cor. 12:30).

15. Interpreting Tongues/Languages—Sometimes, God has enabled one speaker to speak in a foreign language and then enabled another person to interpret the message in the foreign language. Used in combination, these two gifts are similar to prophecy. In other words, if Speaker A gives a message in a foreign language and Speaker B interprets it for everyone, the end result is that a message from God has been given and interpreted.

16. Evangelism/Proclaiming the Good News—All are to be witnesses, but some are especially burdened for it and gifted at it. Evangelists and missionaries proclaim Messiah to the lost and disciple new believers. A person does not have to get paid for and do evangelism full-time to have this gift, though many do. Some of the great evangelists of the past have worked in the marketplace, but have been tremendous witnesses to all around them.

Do you see any areas where you are already serving and feel gifted?

_____

_____

Do you see any areas where you are serving that might not really be your gift? _____

_____

Do you see any areas where you feel a calling or burden and would like to either begin serving or work under someone else to learn?

_____

_____

Homework

Meet with your congregational leader or someone else in leadership. Talk about the areas in which you feel called to serve. Sometimes God may give a new believer one gift until they have grown in the faith and then begin to develop other areas. You are not limited to just one gifting, especially as you mature. Some gifts, such as leadership and teaching, cannot be exercised by new believers in most cases but have to be developed for a few years. If you think this is your area, find a place of service now and begin learning from mature believers who are using those gifts already.

Knowing God's Will

Key Verse: "Whoever does what my Father in heaven wants, that person is my brother and sister and mother." (Matt. 12:50)

Before you came into this walk with Yeshua, it was enough to follow your own will and the will of your loved ones. The only desires you had to consider were your own and those of the people who mattered most to you. Perhaps even then you struggled with the will of others. Maybe the will of your parents was in conflict with your own. A battle of the wills ensued. Perhaps your problem was more subtle—you wanted to do the will of your parents but it was hard to know what would please them.

With God you will not have to worry about clarity. God's will is revealed in the Bible. You can know what God values and what God hates. You can know what sorts of work God desires in his kingdom and what kinds he does not desire. You can know principles for every decision. The will of God has been revealed to men.

Key Scriptures

"Things which are hidden belong to *ADONAI* our God. But the things that have been revealed belong to us and our children forever, so that we can observe all the words of this *Torah*." (Deut. 29:29)

"For this *mitzvah* [commandment] which I am giving you today is not too hard for you, it is not beyond your reach. It isn't in the sky so that you need to ask, 'Who will go up into the sky for us, to bring it to us and make us hear it, so that we can obey it?' Likewise, it isn't beyond the sea, so that you need to ask, 'Who will cross the sea for us, to bring it to us and make us hear it, so that we can obey it?' On the contrary, the word is very close to you—in your mouth, even in your heart; therefore, you can do it!" (Deut. 30:11–14)

"In other words, do not let yourselves be conformed to the standards of the *'olam hazeh* [this world]. Instead, keep letting yourselves be transformed by the renewing of your minds; so that you will know what God wants and will agree that what he wants is good, satisfying, and able to succeed." (Rom. 12:2)

Is God's will a secret, mysterious message that we must get from heaven? _____

Can you find and do God's will? _____

According to Deuteronomy 29:29, where is God's will revealed? _____

According to Deuteronomy 30:11–14, how hard is it to find God's will? _____

According to Romans 12:2, what must you do to know God's will? _____

How can your mind be renewed? _____

Resources For Knowing God's Will

1. Scripture—The most important resource is the Bible. God gave us the Bible in order to reveal his will. This is not a mysterious process. Some people treat the Bible like it is a fortune cookie. When they are seeking an answer, they flip to a random passage for an answer. The story is told of one such person who was looking for God's will. The first passage he flipped to said, "And Judas hanged himself." Puzzled, he tried again and got, "Go and do likewise." Rather than treating the

Bible like a fortune cookie, understand that it is a book showing you who God is and what he expects of you. Learn the
whole Bible, a little at a time, and you will be an expert on
God's will.

2. Prayer—Sometimes decisions are hard. Sometimes we face several options that are all biblical (i.e. no matter which way we
decide we will not go against the teaching of the Bible). In
most of these cases, we cannot go wrong. As long as we are
following God's teaching we will be all right. Nonetheless, it is
always best to pray for guidance in such situations. God can
help us make these decisions in numerous ways. Some people
hear God's voice at times to help them make decisions (but
many, including this writer, have not heard God's voice). Be
open to hearing God's voice. Even if God does not speak to
you, he can make tough decisions easier for you by changing
your circumstances. He may take one of the options away,
closing the door on one of several choices that you had to
make. He may send someone to advise you. Prayer is the second most important factor in knowing God's will.

3. The Congregation and Godly Advisors—When facing decisions that seem unclear or which weigh heavily on you, talk to
your brothers and sisters at the congregation. Sometimes you
may talk with leaders. Sometimes you will not have to ask for
help. Others may approach you, having been burdened by
God to do so, to share with you some insight into your life
choices. Learn to know who the people are in your life who
can give good advice based upon the Scriptures and experience in walking with God. Remember that not all advice is
good advice. If everyone around you disagrees with some decision you have made, they are probably right, but not necessarily. Scripture and prayer are more trustworthy indicators,
but we should not ignore advice.

4. Circumstances—These are the least trustworthy indicators of
God's will, but they are important in certain situations. The
primary ways in which circumstances show us God's will are
opportunities which arise and insurmountable obstacles. Some
people call these open and closed doors. God may provide an
opportunity to talk to someone or to serve in some area that
you had not considered. This circumstance may be God lead-

ing you to do this. On the other hand, you may think that some opportunity is God's will and he will close the door by creating insurmountable obstacles. Circumstances are the least trustworthy means of knowing God's will. Sometimes "insurmountable obstacles" are really just the work of Satan trying to keep us from doing something. Many people have overcome "insurmountable obstacles" when they were sure, through prayer, Scripture, and advice what God's will was. Nonetheless, God will use circumstances to lead us, especially if we are praying for him to.

Can you give an example of God using any or all of these means in your life? _____

_____

_____

_____

Where You Can Go Wrong

There are certain areas where you can fail to obey the will of God. Everyone experiences these failures. Only Yeshua was perfect in following God's will. If you miss God's will, do not worry that you are doomed for the rest of your life. God's will is like a road. You will veer off of it many times, but you can always get back on, no matter how badly you fail. Some primary areas of failure include:

Not serving in the body—God has called all believers to serve in the congregation and in other areas of kingdom work. If you never talk to others about your faith, if you do nothing to help the congregation, if you cannot explain to someone what you are doing for God, then you are not following God's will. Of course, there are some who are physically unable to do much due to health problems. Some may even be totally incapacitated. God is not expecting someone on his death bed to serve in any major way, but other than such extreme cases, you have not been called to be a spectator.

Serving in areas God hasn't called you to—Sometimes a person may serve in wrong areas out of a false humility, "I think God has called me to counsel with others, but I don't feel wise. Instead I serve by helping the physical needs of the congregation." If you are called to teach, counsel, or lead, don't let false humility hold you back. If you are not ready yet, then your calling is at least to be learning. On the other hand, it is common for the opposite situation to occur. Someone may miss her calling because she yearns for one that seems important. If you are called to be a giver, give cheerfully and learn to maximize your ability to give.

Disobeying commandments and going against the Scriptures—The most obvious way to miss God's will is to violate the teaching of the Bible. One woman told me that she was led by God to divorce her husband. "Did he cheat on you? Was he violent?" I asked. She said he was not, but that she just couldn't live with an unbeliever. I knew the Scripture (1 Cor. 7:15) that says that a believer should remain married to an unbeliever unless they want a divorce. I knew this woman had missed God's will.

Holding Ungodly attitudes—Often our failures are not so obvious as disobeying a commandment and taking action that is sinful. Rather, our most common errors in following God's will have to do with attitudes. God's will is that we have love, joy, peace, patience, kindness, goodness, faithfulness, gentleness, and self-control (Gal. 5:22–23). It is all right to mourn when we are bereaved or face difficult challenges. It is all right to be momentarily troubled by hardships. But through prayer and reading the Scriptures, we should be restored to godly attitudes quickly. There is no excuse for hatred, division, and bitterness. We must love even our enemies and leave vengeance to God.

Life Decisions That Are Not So Clear

What do you do about decisions that are not about right and wrong? Should I marry this person? What job should I take? Which house should I buy?

First of all, God's will is not some mysterious plan that must be found through mystical meditation. One does not have to be a monk in solitude and fasting for hours each day seeking a heavenly vision. God's will is more clear than that. You need not fear that you will be out of God's will if you make some subtle error in a decision. God is not going to say to you, "You married the wrong person. I know she was godly and shared in your faith, but I meant for you to marry someone else. You missed my will." If you follow the Scriptures, pray for guidance, and follow godly counsel on major decisions, you cannot go wrong.

In difficult decisions, you should follow these simple steps:

1. Think about what scriptural principles may apply. If you are considering marriage, is your partner a believer who loves and obeys God? If you are buying a house, are you going to put yourself into financial hardship? Are you moving into an area that will make it harder for you to serve God? While there may not be a commandment about the decision you are making, there are often principles that apply.

2. Pray for guidance through circumstances and advice (or, if you are so blessed, through the voice of God speaking to you). Don't make major decisions without some time for prayer.

3. Ask advice from people you trust. There may be scriptural principles that you are unaware of. There may be ramifications to your decision that you haven't thought of. Sometimes it may not even be a "spiritual" issue, but something much more mundane. You may find out that a certain type of job will be bad for your future. You may find out that a potential mate has had a history of problems you knew nothing about. Making major life choices without seeking advice is not wise.

4. Look carefully at your circumstances. God may be leading you and helping make the decision easy for you. If you get an un-usual opportunity, it may be (not necessarily though) because God is blessing you. If there are obstacles to something you want to do, it may be because your desire is selfish and not godly.

If you follow these steps, you cannot really go wrong. If it is important to God that you buy the house on Lincoln Street, he is not going to make it easy for you to buy the one on Elm Street. God does not expect us to be intuitive geniuses who can pick up subtle signs. He loves us and wants us to do his will. He will lead you and guide you like a shepherd, just as he promised.

Homework

Think about several of the life decisions you have made, perhaps recently. How have you used Scripture, prayer, advice, and circumstances to help you? Write out some thoughts about past decisions and any upcoming decisions.

The Greatest Commandment

Key Verse: "And you are to love ADONAI, your God, with all your heart, all your being, and all your resources." (Deut. 6:5)

Perhaps they were hoping that he would discredit himself by answering their question in an unacceptable way. It may be that they were trying to get him involved in a dispute between rival Jewish factions. Or they might have just been curious to know his answer, "Rabbi, which of the *mitzvot* in the *Torah* is the most important?" (Matt. 22:36)

His answer was not any different from the answer that the Jewish establishment in his day would have given. Yet, the sense with which he lived the greatest commandment excels all other teachers before and after him. Yeshua's greatest answer to the question given that day was not just in words, but in a life lived like no other has been lived.

The Commandment Itself

Yeshua answered the inquirer by giving two verses from Deuteronomy and the first part of the Jewish prayer known as the Shema:

> *Sh'ma Yisra'el, ADONAI Eloheinu, ADONAI echad* [Hear, O Isra'el, the LORD our God, the LORD is one], and you are to love ADONAI, your God, with all your heart, with all your soul, with all your understanding and with all your strength (Mark 12:29–30).

Yeshua is quoting Deuteronomy 6:4–5. Whereas the Hebrew text lists three areas in which love for God must dwell (heart, being, and might), the Greek text here lists four (heart, soul, understanding, and strength). This is because the three words in Hebrew encompass everything that these four terms in Greek entail.

The first part of the commandment is a call to Israel to understand that only ADONAI is God, as opposed to the numerous deities that they had worshiped in Egypt and that were worshiped in

Canaan. Some see the main point of the verse being God's oneness (*ADONAI* is one), but the Hebrew might also refer to *ADONAI* being the only God (*ADONAI* alone). Regardless of which meaning is intended, the text suggests that God alone is to be worshipped.

The second part of the commandment is an explanation of what the first part entails. If God alone is to be worshipped, how shall he be worshipped? The answer that is given ought to be seen as the total demand of our lives for God:

> And you shall love *ADONAI*, your God, with all your heart and with all your being, and with all your muchness
>
> *V'ahavta et ADONAI, eloheicha, b'chol l'vavcha, u'vchol naf'sh'cha, uv'chol me'odecha*

The commandment is all-inclusive. This is not just a warm and fuzzy verse about loving God. God is demanding all of three areas of our lives:

1. Heart (*levav*)—This refers to our thinking, feeling, and choosing. In numerous verses in the Hebrew Bible people are shown to think with their heart, to feel, and to make choices. The heart is the mind, emotions, and will.
2. Being (*nefesh*)—Often translated "soul," *nefesh* is actually much more than the Greek concept of soul. The *nefesh* is the whole being, including the body. In some references, corpses are referred to as *nefesh*. The human being can be looked at in individual parts, material (body) and immaterial (soul, mind, feelings, will, etc.). But the overarching truth is that all of these parts fit into one well-made being. That is what the *nefesh* really is, the living being in all its parts.
3. Muchness (*me'od*)—We wouldn't speak this way in English. The idea is that we are to give every ounce of our hearts and beings to God.

Understanding the meaning of the terms in the commandment, consider the meaning of the whole: "You shall love God with all of your thinking, feeling, and choosing—your whole being—with all the intensity that is in you."

Only Yeshua has ever perfectly kept this commandment throughout life. At times all of us have held back some thoughts for ourselves, entertained some feelings that would displease him, and made some decisions that violated his will. Yet, this standard calls us always to get closer to God, to align ourselves more and more with his will, and to cultivate feelings that God desires for us to have.

Loving God With Your Thinking

"How do you love someone in the area of your thoughts?" you might ask. Really this is not so difficult. An analogy will help. You may remember a time when you were getting close to someone, perhaps a romantic interest or a best friend. Often there is a time of discovery in such relationships. You discover new things about your beloved as often as you can. You want to know what life was like for them growing up, what things they love, what things they hate, how they think about a myriad of issues, and how they feel about you. You are getting to know them.

During a discovery period in a relationship, it is amazing how much conversational time there can be and how the time never seems like enough. A telephone call for an hour seems too short. A lunch together couldn't possibly be long enough. You love getting to know them. This is loving someone with your thoughts, wanting to know all about them.

So with God we can take great joy in getting to know him. There is a great deal to learn about God: his unchanging, constant, eternal, loving, just, stern yet kind, transcendent yet near, all-knowing, commanding yet empowering nature. The mysteries of the Trinity and Incarnation can thrill the mind for hours. His ways and will are a never-ending subject of study. It seems that when you get to the end of the Bible, you have forgotten and are ready to return to some of the details from the beginning. When this life is over and we think we have come to know him well, we will appear before him and a whole new, infinite world of knowledge about him will open up to us.

In what ways are you loving God with your thinking these days?

_____

_____

Is there more that you ought to do? What? _____

_____

_____

Loving God With Your Feelings

When a relationship is new, feelings are usually easy to have. A romantic interest or best friend inspires wonderful feelings when things are brand new, but as the relationship matures, we take them for granted more and more. That is, we take them for granted unless we learn to cultivate feelings of love.

Right now, perhaps your relationship with God is new and the feelings of love are strong. In time they can begin to wear down. You run the danger of losing your first love unless you cultivate a sort of holy, romantic love between you and God.

Think about married couples who are older, yet who still love each other deeply and very obviously. What is their secret? Generally it is that they express their love to one another often, they spend a great deal of time together, and they do things together that build their love.

With God, there are many opportunities to express love, privately and in groups. Musical worship is one of the special times. Praising God in song is like dancing with your husband or wife. Musical praise is a time of intimacy between you and God, if you are paying attention. Just as someone can just go through the motions on a romantic date, so it is possible to be apathetic in worship. If your focus is on the beauty of the music or on how your voice sounds, you will miss the beauty of the God you are praising. Worship during private prayer is another way that we can express love for God. Another is to read passages from his word that inspire in us a sense of his beauty and express that back to him in praise as we read. If you do these things often, they will become a habit for you. When your relationship with God gets old, the fire will not be lost.

In what ways are you loving God with your feeling these days? _

_____

_____

_____

Is there more that you ought to do? What? _____

_____

_____

_____

Loving God With Your Choosing

This is without a doubt the hardest area to be consistent in loving God. Yet it is vital. Imagine a husband who talks to his wife often and knows her well; he buys her flowers and candy and takes her dancing, he praises her in front of others as often as possible, and all the while he is cheating on her. When she discovers his infidelity, what will she think of the candy and flowers?

The areas of mind, emotion, and will are interdependent. What you think you will usually choose. What fills you with good emotions will be easy for you to choose. Loving God with our choosing means obeying him. This is a form of love, as Yeshua said, "You are my friends, if you do what I command you" (John 15:14). If you do well at loving God with your thinking and feeling, it will be easier for you to love him with your choices.

One secret to doing well in this area is to obey him in the small things as well as in the large things. Yeshua tells us that we must make the weightier issues of the law a priority (Matt. 23:23). The other side of the coin is that obedience in small things is easy to neglect, yet it is valuable training for obedience in greater things. Yeshua also taught this side of obedience: "Someone who is trustworthy in a small matter is also trustworthy in large ones, and someone who is dishonest in a small matter is also dishonest in large ones" (Luke 16:10). Begin obeying him in small and large things and do it out of love. Fidelity to God is love, just as fidelity to a spouse is love. Let him be the ultimate end of all your desires and lose all self-interest and then you will really know what it is to love God.

In what ways are you loving God with your choosing these days?

_____

_____

_____

_____

Is there more that you ought to do? What? _____

_____

_____

_____

Homework

Write up an evaluation of your love for God in the three key areas, thinking, feeling, and choosing. Make plans to improve your "marriage" with God.

The Great Commission

Key Verse: ". . . so that your way may be known on earth, your salvation among all nations." (Ps. 67:2; verse 3 in Hebrew Bibles)

When the Messiah gives us a job to do, how can we do anything but give our lives to it? The Great Commission is Yeshua's commandment to the whole Body of Messiah worldwide to make disciples from among all mankind. This commission is often neglected, and that has led some to call it "the Great Omission" (Robertson McQuilkin, former president of Columbia Bible College, has a fantastic book by that title; see bibliography).

The Great Commission has been in some ways a success story for the Body of Messiah throughout the ages. The good news of Yeshua has spread to the whole world. At least a part of the Bible has been translated into thousands of languages (with thousands more to go). Truly, people from virtually all tribes, languages, and nations have come to know Yeshua as Messiah (Rev. 7:9). Yet, the story is not completely one of success. Perhaps the greatest disobedience of the Body of Messiah falls in this area of the Great Commission. Fewer and fewer believers are supporting the work of the Great Commission financially. More importantly, too many see the work as someone else's responsibility and few share the good news right where they live and amongst the people with whom they work and live.

Messiah's Commission to His Body

The first thing that is vital to know about Yeshua's commission is that it was not completely new in the time of the apostles. God's desire for all men to know him starts at the very beginning of the Bible. He created us to know him and live in a relationship with him. When men kept turning away from God in the early stories in Genesis, God eventually decided to reveal himself to the world through one people, the descendants of Abraham. His promise is to Abraham was, "I will make of you a great nation, I will bless you and I will make your name great; and you are to be a blessing. I will bless those who bless you, but I will curse those who curse you; and by you all the families of the earth will be blessed" (Gen. 12:2–3). God planned to bless the whole earth through the people of Abraham.

How would God do this? He had always planned for Israel to reveal him to the world. As the Psalmist said:

> Give *ADONAI* his due, you families from among the peoples; give *ADONAI* his due of glory and strength; give *ADONAI* the glory due his name; bring an offering, and enter his courtyards. Worship *ADONAI* in holy splendor; tremble before him, all the earth! Say among the nations, "*ADONAI* is king!" The world is firmly established, immovable. He will judge the peoples fairly. (Ps. 96:7–10)

The peoples mentioned in Psalm 96 are tribes or nations outside of Israel. Psalm 96 is a psalm about spreading the news of *ADONAI* to the nations (see also Psalm 67). There are numerous references in the Psalms to God's name being made known to the nations.

As Yeshua was leaving this world and ascending to be with the Father, he left us some words of instruction that further clarified God's plan to reveal himself to the nations:

> Therefore, go and make people from all nations into *talmidim*, immersing them into the reality of the Father, the Son, and the *Ruach HaKodesh*, and teaching them to obey everything that I have commanded you. (Matt. 28:19–20)

> But you will receive power when the *Ruach HaKodesh* comes upon you; you will be my witnesses, both in Yerushalayim [Jerusalem] and in all Y'hudah and Shomron [Judah and Samaria], indeed to the ends of the earth. (Acts 1:8)

His commission was that we take the good news into the whole world, starting with Israel and spreading out to all nations.

The apostles took this commandment very seriously. Peter and James led the Great Commission in Israel. John led it in Asia Minor. Paul and many others spread the good news all over the Roman Empire. According to later historians, Thomas took the message to India—quite a long journey in those days! All of the apostles, except for John, were killed for their role in spreading the good news. Paul was beheaded and Peter was crucified upside down. They obeyed this commandment even to the death. When the Sanhedrin, the Jewish high court, ordered Peter and John to stop teaching about Yeshua, they replied, "You must judge for yourselves whether it is right in the sight of God for us to listen to you rather than God. As for us, we can't help talking about what we have seen and heard" (Acts 4:19–20).

What level of importance ought we to give the Great Commission and why? _____

_____

_____

_____

The Special Role of Jewish Believers in God's Plan

It is commonly known that Gentiles have a special place in God's plan to reach Jewish people: ". . . it is by means of their [Israel's] stumbling [not accepting Messiah] that the deliverance has come to the Gentiles, in order to provoke them to jealousy" (Rom. 11:11). Gentiles are a witness to Jewish people when they see the love of God in them.

By the same token, Jewish people have always had a calling to reach the Gentiles: "And you will be a kingdom of *cohanim* [priests] for me, a nation set apart" (Exod. 19:6). Priests are those who serve as intermediaries between worshippers and God. The priests in the Temple served as a go-between for the people and God. If all Israel are priests, who are the people for whom they mediate with God? The answer, of course, would have to be those who are not Israel, the nations. Israel was called in the *Torah* to be God's priests to the world.

All believers are supposed to plug into Yeshua's Great Commission, but how much more should a Jewish believer do this! Being a part of God's chosen people, the people through whom God reveals himself to the world, Jewish believers ought to be a part of God's work on the whole earth.

107

Many people have experienced the power of the testimony of a Jewish believer. When a non-believing Gentile meets a Jewish person who has come to faith in Yeshua, he or she tends to stand up and take notice. Why would a person from a people persecuted by Christianity come to faith in Yeshua? Why would a person from a community sworn to reject Yeshua decide instead to believe in him? The world is confounded by your faith and it speaks volumes to them.

Because proclaiming the good news to the Jewish community has been so neglected for centuries, it is natural that Messianic Jewish congregations, Jewish ministries, and individual Jewish believers often focus on Israel and the Jewish community. There is nothing wrong with this. But we also have an opportunity to go beyond Jerusalem and Judea into all the world. What an opportunity to bring God's promise full circle, that "all the nations of the earth will be blessed by you"!

Have you considered the possibility of getting involved in outreach to Gentile peoples and countries? How do you feel about it?

_____

_____

_____

Practical Ways to Join in the Great Commission

1. Support missionaries financially. Your congregation may have a missions offering or they may have a list of missionaries supported by the congregation.

2. Get to know about and pray for specific missionaries. Most have a prayer letter that you can sign up for. When the letters come, pray for them. If you have a family, get your whole family involved.

3. Support and pray for ministries in your own area. Don't just think about people working in other countries. The Great Commission is also for your own community. Pray for the outreach of your congregation. Pray for other ministries that seem to be making a valuable contribution to people coming to know Yeshua.

4. Be ready to share your story of faith and reasons to believe

with others. Don't think this is just for professionals. And consider whether God might be leading you to work in missions either in your area or overseas, amongst the Jewish people or amongst non-Jewish people.

5. Consider helping disciple other new believers after your training is done. You are learning how to walk in the faith. Later, you will be able to teach others, just as you have learned. The Great Commission is not just introducing people to Yeshua, but also training them to obey and live for him.

6. Support the work of your local congregation and especially in outreach. When your congregation holds any event designed to get the message of Yeshua out to those who have not heard, put your support behind it in any way that you can.

7. Learn about other countries and people groups and pray for them. There are a variety of ways you can learn about the needs of other countries. You can get to know a missionary family by signing up for their prayer letter. Through their prayer letters and perhaps some publications from their mission boards you can learn what to pray for. You might also get a book such as *Operation World* by Patrick Johnstone (see bibliography) or even just a good World Atlas.

How might you see yourself getting involved in the Great Commission? _____

_____

_____

_____

Homework

Learn about one missionary family and the country they work in. Pray for them and the needs that they have requested prayer for.

Section

POTENTIAL PROBLEM AREAS

Four

The *Torah* and the Believer

Imagine a Messianic Jewish conference during mealtime. The fellowship around the table, between Jewish and Gentile believers from various parts of the country, is outstanding. As the conversation drifts into the realm of the spiritual, someone asks those around the table, "So, do you all keep Shabbat?"

Immediately a Jewish believer answers, "Oh, yes. We light the candles on Friday night and we never miss Shabbat services on Saturday morning."

A few people at the table nod approvingly. Then a Gentile believer says, "We keep the Sabbath on Sunday and we never miss church."

Several of the table guests exchange suppressed smiles until another Jewish believer speaks up. He is known to be very much like the Orthodox in his practice. "We walk to synagogue on Shabbat." Now most of the guests smile nervously, although at least one returns a clearly impressed grin.

What are the issues in this imaginary conversation? Interestingly, none of the responses to the question concern the *Torah* at all.

So much of the divisive issue of the law and the believer in ordinary conversations isn't really about the *Torah* at all, but about rabbinical traditions and commandments (called the Oral *Torah* by the Orthodox community). The lighting of candles on Friday night and the synagogue service are not in the *Torah*. These are rabbinical customs. It is possible to keep the *Torah* without lighting Shabbat candles. Driving a car on Shabbat is prohibited by the rabbis, but isn't addressed directly in the *Torah*. Nor is the Sabbath in the *Torah* or in the New Testament said to fall on a Sunday. So the participants in this discussion haven't actually touched on the issue of the *Torah* at all.

In this chapter, we will take a look at genuine issues in the *Torah*. In the following chapter, we will look at the believer's position in regard to rabbinical commands and customs.

More Agreement Than We Think

In reality, there is quite a bit more agreement on the *Torah*, the five books of Moses, than we think. Jewish and Gentile believers from most traditions consider many of the commandments in the *Torah* as universally authoritative. When it comes to issues such as adultery, theft, homosexuality, incest, drug use, and idolatry, we all agree the Bible forbids these practices.

However, concerning certain laws in *Torah* that are regarded by some as "ceremonial," people can have disagreements. Major areas of disagreement over the *Torah* would include Shabbat, holy days, dietary laws, and *tzitziyot* (fringes commanded in the *Torah*). How can we decide whether we are bound to keep certain commands in these areas?

Common Views on the *Torah*

In the history of the church, one particular view has been most common regarding the *Torah*. In this traditional view, the *Torah* has been seen as a compendium of laws covering three spheres: moral, ceremonial, and civil. Moral laws, those having to do with issues of ethics and righteousness, are still valid and authoritative today. The ceremonial laws, having to do with ritual purity, with a Tabernacle/Temple, with a priesthood, with animal sacrifices, and with holy days and sabbaths, are null and void. Likewise, all laws concerning the operation of Israel's civil government are null and void. These laws, though not directly applicable, remain for us as a revelation of God's character.

Interpreters have long seen problems with this traditional view. God did not give the *Torah* in neat categories like moral, civil, and ceremonial. He simply gave laws.

Martin Luther held a view quite different from the traditional Christian one. He claimed that none of the law is authoritative, since to be subject to one part of the law would put us under its whole authority. Not even the so-called "moral laws" held any weight for the believer. Rather, Luther saw the *Torah* as a unified code of law that could not be separated. He did believe in a law of God, which is not the same as the law of Moses. This law of God is not the gospel, but a tool to lead us to the gospel. By realizing we cannot keep the law of God, we are forced to turn to the gospel of faith. The law of Moses reflects God's eternal law, but its statutes must be confirmed in other parts of Scripture to hold any weight for the believer.

A very common view in modern times shares the Lutheran view that none of the *Torah* is binding. Dispensationalism, a position that began in the late nineteenth century, teaches that the *Torah* was a covenant treaty with Israel, rather like a constitution. Israel has dissolved as a theocratic nation (the modern state is not a theocracy, but a democracy). Therefore, the constitution has been dissolved as well. Therefore, no one is bound by even one of its laws. They all remain as revelation, as teachings that reveal God's will in some places and that reveal his character in others. But the *Torah* has no authority at all in the life of a believer. God does have a universal law, not to be confused with a written law code, that we as believers are bound to keep. But God's universal law is expressed in the teachings of the apostles and not in the *Torah*.

Another Way of Looking at the *Torah*

These common views demonstrate some of the range of choices we have in deciding how to deal with the *Torah*. We might accept part of the *Torah* as authoritative, or none of it. Perhaps this raises the question, "Can't we accept all of it?"

The clear answer to this is, "It's not possible!" Even the Orthodox Jewish community recognizes this. According to Orthodox *halakhah* (official decisions about how to keep the commandments), there are 613 commandments and prohibitions in *Torah*. A modern compilation of this *halakhah* called *The Taryag Mitzvos* (613 Commandments) shows clearly that the rabbis consider only 375 of the 613 commandments to be applicable today.[10] The rabbis have even less reason than followers of Yeshua to consider commandments inapplicable today, and they admit that many of the commandments do not apply.

The simple reason that some say some of the commandments are inapplicable is that our situation as readers of the *Torah* has changed considerably since the time that Moses gave it. There is no theocracy of Israel. Moreover, Yeshua, in his atoning death and in his High Priesthood, has fulfilled the Temple, priestly, and sacrificial systems. Therefore, laws in these areas are not binding for modern believers.

When the rabbis consider *halakhah*, they do not divide the *Torah* into categories like the traditional view in the church. Rather, they look at each law individually and assess whether or not it can be applied today. Perhaps this is what should be done.

How To Decide About Laws in the *Torah*

For any commandment we read about in *Torah*, we must ask several questions. What is the purpose of the commandment? Has Yeshua's atoning death rendered the commandment unnecessary? Can the commandment be applied today in keeping with God's purpose in giving it? Is the commandment in some way limited in application to systems that no longer exist?

As examples, let's apply this to a few laws. In Leviticus 6:4 (5:23 in Hebrew Bibles), we read that thieves should give back what they have stolen as a part of their restitution. This commandment occurs in the middle of a large section on animal sacrifices. Someone who is prone to divide the law into categories might throw this commandment out immediately because it's found among the ceremonial laws. The purpose of this commandment is that the offender would properly repent of the sin of stealing. To complete that repentance, it is necessary to return the stolen item. Can this be applied today? Absolutely; there is no reason that a thief today could not be expected to return stolen items as part of his repentance.

On the other hand, in Leviticus 25:23, we read that land in Israel is not to be sold permanently. Can a follower of Messiah, living in Israel today, sell property? To answer this, we have to look at the purpose of Leviticus 25:23. Under the theocratic government of Israel, the land was divided among tribes and families. The land was supposed to stay in the possession of tribes and families forever. Land could be leased until the next Sabbath year, but could never be sold permanently. Clearly, the system of tribal land ownership cannot be applied today, since the theocracy of Israel is dissolved and since the tribes cannot be determined today. Therefore, this law cannot be applied. (The rabbis agree.)

What About Shabbat and the Holy Days?

Most believers, both Jewish and Gentile, have a poor understanding of the Shabbat laws. Most people associate the Shabbat law with worship services. Scripturally, this idea that worship services are to be held on Shabbat is based upon Leviticus 23:3, which says that a "sacred assembly" is to be held on each Shabbat. What is the meaning of this assembly and to whom did it apply? Did the believers in ancient Israel go to synagogue on Shabbat? The answer is, "No." There were no synagogues. Did they come to the Tabernacle or Temple each Shabbat? Again, the answer is, "No." Who then comes to this sacred assembly? Whenever the sacred assembly is mentioned in Leviticus 23, immediately following the phrase is a description of the kinds of offerings that are to be made in the Tabernacle/Temple (except after verse 3). On Shabbat, the priests had to bring new consecrated bread into the sanctuary and offer double sacrifices. The "sacred assembly" was a duty of the priests rather than a duty for the people as a whole.

If God doesn't command us to worship on Shabbat, then what is its purpose? The answer, in all of the Shabbat commandments in Scripture, is clear: Shabbat is for rest. Work, other than ministering to the needs of others, and commerce are forbidden on Shabbat. Is this applicable today? Did Yeshua fulfill Shabbat? It seems that the Bible bases the commandment to rest on Shabbat upon the Creation order, where God rested on the seventh day. Therefore, Shabbat is not superceded by Yeshua's sacrifice, but applies to the whole created order. It is not a temporary commandment, but a permanent one.

Believers in Yeshua can worship on Shabbat (a study of the New Testament will show that Sunday is not a mandatory day of worship either) or on any day of the week. But we do not have the freedom to mow our lawn or to catch up on work from the office. Professions involving emergency care are lawful on Shabbat since Yeshua taught that it is lawful to heal and to help those in dire need on Shabbat.

With regard to the Holy Days, such as Passover, we can apply the same principles. Some parts of the Holy Days are clearly nonapplicable today. God no longer accepts animal sacrifices, since Yeshua has fulfilled them. But we can keep the special Shabbats of the Holy Days and we can remember and celebrate what God has done on them. To fail to celebrate what God has done for us would be ingratitude.

117

What About the Dietary Laws?

Leviticus 11 prohibits Israel from consuming certain kinds of meat. In modern Orthodox Jewish life, the rabbis have adopted many dietary laws that are not found in the Bible (most notably the issue of mixing milk and meat). Can a believer today eat pork or shrimp?

Finding the purpose of the dietary laws in Leviticus 11 is no easy matter. Many commentators have suggested health as the purpose. The problem with this view is that some of the prohibited foods are actually lower in fat and cholesterol than some of the permitted foods. And of course, the *Torah* does not name health as the purpose. It is quite likely that the dietary laws of Israel made better sense to the original audience than they do to us. There were, perhaps, concerns about purity that we do not understand today.

Since the purpose of the dietary laws is not perfectly clear, there will always be room for disagreement on the issue of what believers today can and cannot eat. However, there is some evidence to suggest that the dietary laws were a part of a system that may be inapplicable today, the clean/unclean system.

In ancient Israel, if you touched a corpse, you were unclean for seven days (Num. 19:12). Similarly, those who touched any of the unclean animals described in the dietary laws would be unclean until evening (Lev. 11:24). Is the clean/unclean system rendered obsolete by Yeshua? Perhaps. First, we are rendered eternally clean by accepting his sacrifice for our sins. Therefore we cannot become unclean. Second, being unclean would have no meaning today anyway. Uncleanness was not synonymous with sin in the *Torah*. It is not a sin to touch a corpse (especially not if it is a loved one). A person in a state of uncleanness merely had to avoid holy areas and holy objects so as not to defile them, and to engage in a cleansing ritual. Holy areas and objects do not exist today.

Therefore, one could argue that a Jewish believer who eats shrimp or pork would not be sinning. Some could argue to the contrary. They might point to the words of Leviticus 11, which says that "touching" an unclean animal makes one unclean. The text does not say what happens to those who "eat" an unclean animal, but simply forbids it. Therefore, it is permissible, by this argument, to touch a corpse or to handle an unclean animal today, but not to eat it. Nonetheless, there is no Scripture in the New Testament which cancels the dietary laws (although some people interpret several verses this way).

Regardless of which position you take, one thing is clear: It is not sinful to abstain from unclean foods by choice. As a believer in Yeshua, you are not required to eat ham to show your freedom in Messiah. And there are numerous valid reasons why a Jewish believer might voluntarily give up unclean food: belief that it is forbidden; witness to the Jewish community; longtime habit of avoiding unclean food; or sensitivity to friends and loved ones.

What About *Tzitziyot?*

Tzitziyot are the fringes worn on the corner of the garments in obedience to the commandment in Numbers 15:38. These tassels are to be worn "throughout all generations." There are arguments for and against the requirement of *tzitziyot* today.

The purpose of the *tzitziyot* is to remind one of God's commandments. Their design is well-suited to the form of dress that the ancient Israelites wore. The modern version of *tzitziyot*, worn by the Orthodox, is a modification of the original idea to accommodate modern clothing.

Arguments for requiring *tzitziyot* today would include the fact that the commandment is "throughout all generations" and that the purpose of the *tzitziyot* is still valid for today. Those who argue against requiring them would point out that *tzitziyot* were designed as another law to keep Israel separate from the nations. Today, Jewish and Gentile believers are not separate. Each believer has to decide for himself whether *tzitziyot* are required today or not. If a believer does wear them, he must not do so with an attitude of superiority. Nor should anyone subject a believer who wears *tzitziyot* to a charge of "legalism," since the issue of their requirement is unclear.

For more on *tzitziyot*, see the next chapter, "The Believer and Rabbinical Customs."

What If Others Say I am Legalistic?

Without a doubt, anyone who keeps a commandment such as Shabbat will eventually be charged by someone with legalism. If anyone makes this claim to you, ask them to define legalism. The truth is, many who use this label cannot define it.

There are really two definitions of legalism. One is much more serious than the other. On the one hand, there is heretical legalism (heretical means outside of the faith). Heretical legalism is the idea that keeping commandments or the doing of good deeds earns salvation (salvation by works). Clearly, keeping God's commandments is not heretical legalism. No one who avoids adultery out of love for and obedience to God is guilty of heretical legalism. We obey because we are saved, not in order to be saved.

The other kind of legalism involves making additional rules that are stricter than God's laws and then requiring them of ourselves and others. The rabbis frequently engaged in this type of legalism. They saw that stricter laws would prevent transgression of lesser laws. The decision to keep Shabbat opens one up to such a charge, for most believers today do not believe that the Shabbat commandments are still in effect. If you keep Shabbat, don't be surprised when some well-meaning believer accuses you of being a "Judaizer" or of being legalistic.

The way to answer this charge is simple. What is at issue is not really legalism, but a difference in interpretation of Scripture. Simply point this out. Explain that you are keeping Shabbat out of love for God, not to earn his favor (which you already have in Yeshua). Explain that you believe the commandment to keep Shabbat is the same as the commandment to avoid adultery. You are just obeying God and not trying to keep human rules and regulations.

Summary

Knowing which commandments in the *Torah* apply to believers today is a difficult task. The rabbis have devoted many books to the subject. Unfortunately, the Christian world has paid little attention to this issue, other than in a theoretical sense. As believers in Yeshua, we need to think carefully about all of God's commandments (in the *Torah* and in the rest of the Bible) and decide how to apply them.

It is not legalistic to keep God's commandments with the right attitude. There is no superiority or lording it over others who disagree with our interpretation. There is no sense of earning God's favor. Proper obedience is given out of love rather than to earn favor.

The Believer and Rabbinical Customs

"Do you just interpret the Bible for yourself, or do you consult the great writings of the rabbis to get your interpretation?" the angry student asked me. "If you're not reading the rabbis, you're not even a player," he said, dismissing as invalid anything else I had to say. It was my first experience of being snubbed by someone from the Orthodox Jewish persuasion. His words have stayed with me because they get to the heart of the matter—is it Bible or is it tradition?

Many Messianic Jewish practices, including *yarmulkes,* Passover seders, prayer books, Shabbat candles, and Hanukkah menorahs come from ancient Jewish tradition and the teaching of the rabbis. To be sure, Yeshua and the Apostles clearly followed some of these customs, such as the Passover Seder. Yet many practices at the heart of a Jewish home are not biblical commandments but come from what is known as the Oral *Torah.*

Did you ever wonder what Moses was doing up on Mt. Sinai for 40 days and nights? The rabbis say that he was receiving numerous additional commandments and applications of the *Torah* from the mouth of God. God commanded that Moses not write these down, but rather pass them on verbally to his seventy elders who would pass them on the next generation, and so on. These verbal commandments of God are the basis of the Oral *Torah* (*Pirke Avot* 1:1).

Following the destruction of the Temple and the defeat of the Jewish uprisings against Rome, the ancient scholars became convinced that teachings from the Oral *Torah* would be lost. Therefore, around 200 C.E. they wrote down the most important issues in a book, the *Mishnah.* The Mishnah records dialogues and debates between the rabbis about how to keep the law in a variety of situations. Through these dialogues, the rabbis arrive at a consensus about how the law is specifically to be kept. The consensus they arrive at on any issue is believed to be one and the same with the Oral *Torah* Moses received. In other words, the decisions that the rabbis come to reflect the best and most accurate of what was passed down by word of mouth from Moses.

Around 500 C.E., a large commentary was added to the Mishnah, called the *Gemara.* It contains much additional material covering ground not touched on in the Mishnah. These two together are called the *Talmud*. The Oral *Torah* is primarily to be found in the Talmud, although certain other opinions of the rabbis, such as the Tosefta, also are said to be repositories of the Oral *Torah*. Rabbinical customs are generally rooted in this Oral *Torah*.

Is There an Oral *Torah*?

The Bible does have a few things to say to answer this question. In Deuteronomy 31:24, we read that Moses "kept writing the words of this *Torah* in a book until he was done." He didn't leave out some of God's commandments, but wrote them all. In Deuteronomy 30:10, he promises a blessing to those who follow the commandments "which are written in this book of the *Torah*." God's commandments are written and left to us in his word. And in Deuteronomy 29:29 (verse 28 in Jewish Bibles), Moses says that the hidden things belong to God, "but the things which have been revealed belong to us," so that "we can observe the words of this *Torah* forever." God has revealed in writing the *Torah* he wants us to observe.

Yeshua warned against people making human ideas into divine commandments. Some experts in the *Torah* came to him and asked why his disciples did not follow the prevailing view of the Oral *Torah* in their day. Yeshua answered with a question, in good Jewish fashion, "Why do you break the command of God by your tradition?" (Matt. 15:3) He then gives us an example in which the rabbinical commandment contradicted one of the Ten Commandments. He finished with these words, "Thus by your tradition you make null and void the word of God!" (Matt. 15:6)

This is not to say that Yeshua was condemning all rabbinical tradition. Most of the rabbinical customs and commandments do not contradict Scripture. But a principle forms the core of Yeshua's response to the issue of traditions of men: the written word is what really counts. God's commandments are written, not passed down orally.

Three Kinds of Rabbinical Customs

One helpful way to evaluate the importance of rabbinical customs is to divide them into three categories:

1. Customs consistent with biblical truth and practiced by Yeshua and the Apostles.
2. Customs consistent with biblical truth.
3. Customs in conflict with biblical truth.

Obviously rabbinical customs from the third category cannot be treated in the same way as the first two. Nor is a custom unaffected by the fact that the Scriptures record Yeshua's participation in them.

We read in the New Testament that Yeshua and the Apostles observed certain rabbinical customs. Yeshua attended synagogue regularly and read from the prophets at the *bimah* (the platform, or pulpit), according to the rabbinical custom of Haftarah readings (Luke 4:16–17). Nowhere in *Torah* (or the prophets) will you find mention of synagogue services or of special readings from the Bible such as the Haftarah reading that Yeshua read. Also, in Luke's account of the Last Supper, we read of Yeshua blessing bread and wine, dipping matzah (unleavened bread), and partaking in a Passover seder (Luke 22). Reading through the commandments regarding Passover in the *Torah*, there is no mention of special cups, of matzah dipped in bitter herbs, of reclining at the meal, or of special blessings. The Bible simply commands people to eat a lamb whole, with bitter herbs and unleavened bread, and to recount the story of Passover to their children. Yeshua and the disciples participated in a Jewish ceremony that contains more tradition than commandment.

Customs blessed by Yeshua's participation in them are a part of our heritage as his followers. Deciding not to participate in such customs will not violate God's will. But participating in them will bring a follower of Yeshua closer to him. These customs might be said to be commended by Yeshua's practice of them.

Many rabbinical customs are not mentioned as having been practiced by Yeshua and the disciples. In fact, many of them were formed after the first century. Yet most are consistent with biblical truth. The *yarmulke* (skullcap) worn by Jewish men as a sign of their submission to God's authority is an example of a rabbinical custom not practiced by Yeshua, but consistent with biblical truth. Those who practice such customs are definitely not doing wrong, and neither are those who do not practice them.

On the other hand, Yeshua opposed certain customs from the Oral *Torah*. In some cases, the customs Yeshua opposed are no longer a part of Jewish practice. Others remain in modern Jewish *halakhah*. One custom Yeshua spoke against was the ritual handwashing, when it might be performed with self-righteous overtones of presumed cleanness before God.

Some teachings of the Oral *Torah* in Yeshua's day were particularly offensive. In some places, the Oral *Torah* finds ways of getting around the Written Law. In the first century, there was a ruling that swearing by the Temple was permitted, but not swearing by the gold of the Temple (Matt. 23:16). There are also teachings in the Oral *Torah* that contradict the truth we know of through Yeshua and the Apostles. For example, in numerous places, the Talmud teaches that prayer, repentance, and good deeds can bring forgiveness for sin apart from blood sacrifice. This directly contradicts Moses and the Prophets, not to mention Yeshua and the Apostles.

How Should the Believer Regard the Oral *Torah*?

Some make a case that believers should keep the Oral *Torah*. There is a passage in Matthew 23:2–3 that could lead one to believe that this is God's desire:

> "The *Torah*-teachers and the *P'rushim* [Pharisees]," he said, "sit in the seat of Moshe [Moses]. So whatever they tell you, take care to do it. But don't do what they do, because they talk but don't act!"

As Dr. David Stern comments in the *Jewish New Testament Commentary* (see bibliography), some "understand this verse to mean that, according to Yeshua, the Oral *Torah*, as expounded in Orthodox Judaism, is binding on Messianic Jews today" (p. 67). This would lead to an odd conclusion.

If the Oral *Torah* is authoritative for today, then Jewish believers and perhaps all believers are supposed to follow the rabbis. That would not only mean no cheeseburgers (from the rabbinical prohibition of eating milk and meat together) but would also mean blood atonement is unnecessary. Those who maintain that Yeshua is validating the Oral *Torah* must in some way explain how parts of the Oral *Torah* that contradict the Bible should be handled.

But it is unnecessary to have to answer such questions. There are certainly other ways to interpret Yeshua's words. David Stern himself takes the passage as meaning that believers before Yeshua's death and resurrection had to follow the Oral *Torah*, but that after Yeshua's resurrection, the Apostles and future leaders in the Body of Messiah would set the interpretation of the commandments for the messianic community (*JNTC* p. 58). Thus, according to his view, the New Testament and the teachings of leaders in the community of believers should be organized into a modern *halakhah*, a formal teaching on how to interpret and keep the biblical commands.

But there is also another way to interpret Yeshua's words. According to the Apostles, the authority of civil governments is binding upon believers as long as it does not violate God's commands. Paul says in Romans 13:1 that we are to "obey the governing authorities," a command backed up by Peter (1 Pet. 2:13). In Yeshua's day, the scribes and Pharisees held great sway in the Sanhedrin, a Jewish court that held some of the power of civil government in Israel. Therefore, Yeshua probably meant that the people were to obey the laws of the Pharisees and scribes as a part of the law of the land. With this understanding, Yeshua was not saying the Oral *Torah* is binding on us today. Nor was he calling for a "New Testament Oral *Torah*." He was merely saying that their legal rulings and judicial decisions were part of a government to be obeyed.

With this theological foundation, let's return to the three different categories of laws from the Oral *Torah*. First, there are the customs and laws of the rabbis that contradict the teaching of the Bible. This area would especially include rabbinical teachings about the afterlife and about atonement, but would also include certain practices. One example is the rabbinical law of conversion to Judaism. According to the rabbis, a person who undergoes a conversion process, including immersion in water, is then Jewish. The Bible defines Jewishness by blood descent from the line of Abraham (Gen. 15:5). Therefore, rabbinical conversions have no weight in the community of faith in Yeshua. Nor is there any reason for Gentiles in the Messianic movement to be "converted" to Judaism. This will not make them Jewish in God's eyes (nor in the rabbis' eyes, since they don't accept Messianic conversions). Rabbinical practices and teachings that conflict with the Bible are to be rejected by believers.

Customs consistent with the Bible and practiced by Yeshua, on the other hand, have a special place in the life of his followers. The Passover seder is one custom that is in part enjoined upon all believers. The bread and wine of communion come from the Passover seder known as the Last Supper. Customs such as the seder and special readings from the prophets, as in Luke 4:16–17, are a part of our heritage. In practicing them, by free choice and not by compulsion, we are participating in part of the life of Yeshua and the Apostles. Clearly these practices, endorsed by Yeshua, are not only acceptable to God, but pleasing.

As for the rest of rabbinical customs, they are neither required nor forbidden. All traditions of faith have customs. Various denominations of Christendom have their own unique customs and traditions. These traditions all have value, provided they agree with Scripture. When a Protestant Christian worships on Sunday morning, purposefully honoring the raising of Yeshua, he is honoring God. When an Anglican Christian prays from the Book of Common Prayer, he honors God. We don't all have to worship on Sunday or pray the Book of Common Prayer, but those who do are pleasing God with traditions that honor him. Likewise, it is pleasing to God when a Messianic Jewish believer prays from the *siddur* and comes up to the *bimah* to read the *Torah* portion of the week. Yet it is not a sin of omission to decline to participate in *siddur* prayers and weekly *Torah* portions.

Traditions can become sin when we require them as though they are commandments. "At that Messianic temple they don't even have a *Torah* scroll," someone says derisively. Suddenly a tradition meant to honor God has become a loathsome opportunity for self-righteousness. Turning human traditions into divine commandments is a form of sin known as legalism.

Does a Jewish Believer Have to Keep Jewish Rabbinical Traditions?

Unfortunately, something as beautiful as Jewish tradition can lead to pride and division. Some people in the Messianic movement are of the opinion that all Jewish believers should keep most or all of rabbinical customs. *Mezuzahs*, prayer shawls, and *yarmulkes* become required.

Part of this argument is the idea that Jewish believers should maintain a Jewish identity. Some even suggest that if a Jewish believer doesn't keep all of these customs he is abetting Satan in his plan to rid the world of Jewish people! Some clear thinking about what makes a person Jewish is required here. By some definitions, Moses wouldn't have been considered Jewish. He never went to synagogue, never said the *Amidah* (the central, "standing" prayer said in synagogues), and didn't wear a *yarmulke* (headcoverings were only for the priests).

There is a far better measure of a person's loyalty to the Jewish people than the Oral *Torah*. The better measure is the *Torah* and the whole Bible. Jewish people who become followers of Yeshua can display their commitment to Jewishness by keeping Shabbat and the holidays and by keeping alive the history and legacy of the Jewish people. They may also choose to participate in many or a few of the rabbinical customs as a way of keeping that legacy.

Is it possible for a Jewish person then to assimilate and withdraw from the Jewish community? Yes, and sadly, many have done this. Many people today with very Jewish last names will say that they are not Jewish. In generations past their family "converted" (the term they will use) to Christianity. In their minds, this means they are now Gentiles. They no longer find a connection with the children of Abraham. Denying one's Jewishness, even if it's done to avoid persecution, is turning one's back on God, who chose the Jewish people as his very own. Yet Jewishness is not a matter of *yarmulkes* and *mezuzahs*, but of biblical obedience and legacy.

If you think about it, most Jewish people in the world today do not wear *yarmulkes*, have *mezuzahs* on their door, or light Shabbat candles. A Jewish believer in Yeshua who keeps Shabbat biblically, and who raises a family in the legacy of the Jewish people is clearly less assimilated than a secular Jew. The Oral *Torah*, with its many rabbinical customs and traditions, is not the measure of Jewishness. On the other hand, a Jewish believer should not be discouraged from participating by choice in any Jewish tradition that is consistent with Scripture.

In the end, it seems best to avoid extremes. To act as though traditions are commandments is clearly wrong. To avoid traditions as though they were sins is also wrong. To base one's Jewishness on rabbinical customs is wrong, but so is basing one's "faith" on avoiding rabbinical customs. To make Jewishness, as defined by rabbinical customs, a higher priority than submission to God's written commandments is also wrong, just as denying one's Jewish identity is an insult to God. But keeping the commandments and participating freely in beautiful, God-honoring traditions is never wrong.

Tongues and Spirit Baptism

You're standing in a quiet worshipful moment, when suddenly someone begins speaking in a staccato, machine-gun babble that you don't understand. Asking others about it later, you're told that they were "speaking in tongues" or using a "prayer language." In his book *The Beauty of Spiritual Language*, Jack Hayford notes that many people are against the public use of tongues (or any use at all) because of offensive, worship-ruining moments like the one described.

On the other side of this issue, perhaps you have been with a group of believers, praying together in awe of God's holiness. One or two in your group can be heard muttering beautiful syllables under their breath that add intensity and beauty to the group prayer experience. After the "amen" is said, someone pipes up, "I can't believe you guys were doing that 'tongues' thing. Don't you know that gifts have ceased, according to 1 Corinthians 13?"

With the issue of speaking in tongues, we have a spiritual hot potato. Some people swear by it and others swear at it. There are sincere, godly people who believe that they speak in angelic or human languages during prayer and others who believe that the gift of tongues is not active today. Especially in the Messianic Jewish community, we have to learn to get along and to agree to disagree on some issues while working together for the kingdom.

What Does it Mean to Speak in Tongues?

In Greek (and also in Hebrew), languages are called tongues. Speaking in tongues means speaking in languages. In the context of spiritual gifts and of prayer, speaking in tongues means using a language that is unknown to the speaker. Many people believe that there are two kinds of gifts of speaking in tongues:

1. The God-given ability to speak a foreign language for the purpose of revealing God to speakers of that language.
2. The God-given ability to pray in a foreign language or special angelic language not used by men.

The first recorded incident of speaking in tongues happened on *Shavu'ot* (Pentecost) in Acts 2, where the believers were suddenly able to speak in the languages of people from all over the Roman empire. This is speaking in tongues of the first kind. Paul says in 1 Corinthians 14:14, "For if I pray in a tongue, my spirit does pray, but my mind is unproductive." The clear meaning of this chapter is that tongues can be used as a prayer language. This does not mean that we should try to speak in foreign languages, for Luke says that God enables the believer to speak (Acts 2:4). If God wants you to pray in a language unknown to you, he will enable you.

What Should I Believe About Tongues?

This issue is one that people are divided on. You will be pressured by some to speak in tongues and pressured by others not to. Don't allow anyone to pressure you to do anything that God is not leading you to do. Nor should you let anyone keep you from doing something that you are sure God is leading you to do (which should always be consistent with the Bible).

The biblical information is that the gift of tongues and praying with tongues were a common practice in the early congregations. Some people say either that this gift has ceased or that it doesn't seem to be active right now. It is well to dismiss from the start two extremes that are clearly not biblical: that the gift of tongues is said to have ceased in 1 Corinthians 13:8; and that anyone who does not speak in tongues is a second-class follower of Yeshua. Neither extreme is correct.

Those who say that the gift has ceased during the time of the apostles cite 1 Corinthians 13:8, which says that "tongues will cease." The problem with this interpretation is that the context of the passage is clearly the future kingdom of the Messiah. The gift of tongues will not be in use in the life to come, but that doesn't say anything about the present. There is no biblical reason to believe that the gift of tongues has been done away with.

Those who say that all believers should speak in tongues use the stories in the book of Acts. Every time the Spirit came upon believers for the first time in Acts, they spoke in tongues. Therefore, many people say that those who do not speak in tongues have not been baptized with the Spirit. They are second-class believers. Paul is clear, however, that not all believers will speak in tongues (1 Cor. 12:30). Nor does Paul seem to indicate that spiritual maturity is evidenced by the gift of tongues. In fact, the message of 1 Corinthians 12–14 is clear: The gift of tongues is one of the lesser gifts and the Corinthian believers who used it were guilty of spiritual immaturity. Spiritual gifts are given to all believers, the mature and the immature.

All of this can be quite confusing to a new follower of Yeshua. It is obvious at times that people get very emotional about this issue. Some people will shun you if you do not agree with them about the gift of tongues. Should you speak in tongues? The answer, quite simply, is: If God leads you to, then do speak in tongues, but if God does not lead you, don't try to fake it.

If God is not leading you to pray in unknown languages and someone pressures you, just say, "God hasn't led me to do that." Sometimes people will give you some syllables in other languages to say and ask you to repeat them over and over until you learn to speak in tongues. Don't fall for it. This is not consistent with the Scripture that says that God enables you to speak in tongues (Acts 2:5). If God gives you some syllables, follow his lead, but if people give you syllables, don't accept a fake.

If you do speak in tongues and someone is disturbed by it, then consider that you might be doing it in a manner that is disruptive. Paul says that disruption of worship is never the purpose of the gift of tongues (1 Cor. 14:32–33). On the other hand, if you have not been disruptive and the offended person just doesn't like the gift of tongues, say something like, "God probably hasn't led you to do this. He leads his followers into different gifts. But this is something God has led me to do. I hope you can understand that."

What is "Baptism in the Spirit"?

"Baptism in the Spirit" is the spiritual reality pictured in the physical ceremony of water immersion (*tvilah*). In *tvilah*, the believer is pictured as being buried with Yeshua and raised to new life. It is a ceremony of inclusion in the congregation and in the new life found in Messiah. Spirit baptism refers to the spiritual reality of that physical ceremony, inclusion in God's kingdom. It is being moved out of the realm of the physical into the realm of the spiritual. (Eph. 1:3, 20).

There is a debate about the timing of Spirit baptism. Some people believe that after you come to know Messiah, there will come another time when you realize your sinfulness and your need to obey Yeshua in all things. At this time, you will become immersed in the Spirit. Many believe that it is only at this point that you will be able to speak in tongues. Others say that Spirit baptism happens right when you accept Yeshua.

The reason for the debate is that some Scriptures suggest that Spirit baptism could be delayed until some time after salvation while others indicate that it happens at salvation. For example, in Acts 1:5, we read Yeshua saying to the Apostles, "you will be immersed in the *Ruach HaKodesh*" (Holy Spirit). Clearly, Spirit baptism happened some time after salvation for the Apostles. Yet we read in 1 Corinthians 12:13 that all are immersed into one body by one Spirit.

One simple explanation of this difference is that the Spirit baptism of the Apostles was delayed until the *Shavu'ot* after Yeshua had ascended into heaven. This was done so that the whole world, through all those gathered in Jerusalem who would later return to their homes, would see the work of God (Acts 2:5). But now Spirit baptism happens when we believe in Yeshua and are saved.

Those who speak of Spirit baptism happening after salvation may still have a point. Some people believe that after salvation there comes a time when we get a deeper realization of the holiness of God. We make a deeper commitment to Yeshua and after that experience, we walk more closely with him and in deeper obedience. Others believe that there is no one experience of committing more deeply to Yeshua's lordship, but that there will be many experiences. Nonetheless, those who say that the baptism of the Spirit is a second work by God in the life of a believer after salvation may be right in principle if not in terminology. Perhaps what they refer to as Spirit baptism is really a time after salvation when a believer submits more deeply to God and commits to greater holiness. This could include discovering spiritual gifts, such as tongues, but doesn't necessarily have to result in that.

To summarize this confusing issue, there are two views on the timing of Spirit baptism: at salvation or sometime after. The Scriptures indicate that Spirit baptism happens at salvation and that all believers are Spirit baptized from the moment they believe. Yet there are other works that God does in a person's life after salvation. Some believe there is one special time, which is often referred to as being "wholly sanctified." Others believe there will be many times when God calls us to a deeper walk and we respond. The important issue is that there are not two kinds of followers of Yeshua: those who have been Spirit baptized and those who have not. But there are believers who are at different levels of maturity and at different levels of using their gifts.

Section

A MESSIANIC JEWISH LIFESTYLE

Five

Introduction

As a Jewish believer, you have, no doubt, been subject to pressure to be more Jewish and also to be less Jewish. Some people in the Messianic Jewish world have probably encouraged you to be very Orthodox in your practice: pray the *siddur*, wear a *kippah* and *tzitzit*, walk to congregation, and other Orthodox practices. Other well-meaning friends, perhaps non-Jewish Christians, have suggested that such things are "legalistic" or "Judaizing" and suggested that you really ought to come to their church.

One of the biggest debates is whether or not it is right for a Jewish believer to worship in a church rather than a Messianic congregation, and vice-versa. People who debate this miss the relevant issues. God has made the Jewish and Gentile elements in the body of Messiah into one new man (Eph. 2:14). Of course non-Jewish and Jewish believers can worship together. The real issue is the continuing importance of Jewish identity in the life of a Jewish believer.

What a shame it would be if a Jewish person, coming into a relationship with the Jewish Messiah, were to assimilate into non-Jewish, mainstream culture! What a shame if the children or grandchildren of Jewish believers no longer considered themselves Jewish. Messianic congregations make it easier to identify with Jewish culture, there is no doubt about that. Jewish believers worshipping in non-Jewish congregations will have to work all the harder to maintain Jewish identity. But the real issue is not where you worship.

The following section is intended to help you understand your Jewish tradition. Keep in mind that Jewish identity is primarily a matter of the home, not the congregation. This section is intended only as an introduction to these elements of Messianic Jewish lifestyle. Further reading will be helpful. I recommend *God's Appointed Times* and *God's Appointed Customs* by Barney Kasdan to help you more fully understand these practices (see bibliography).

Shabbat

In the movie *Fiddler on the Roof*, the milkman Tevye is coming home from a difficult day of delivering milk. His wife is shouting at him, "Hurry up, you'll be late!" He keeps responding, "I won't be late, I won't be late!" The frenetic preparations and the hustling and bustling then suddenly come to a close as Tevye dons a special robe for the Shabbat table and his wife lights the candles. Suddenly the movie is in one of its most beautiful scenes as the family joins together in the prayers for Shabbat.

Shabbat, or Sabbath, is an oasis. A literal oasis is water in the desert. Shabbat is water in the spiritual desert. The commandment is not to *do* something, but to rest. This commandment is not for the Jewish people only, but for all who follow God. Shabbat is a way of honoring God and restoring the body.

Is Shabbat for Today?

As I said before, Shabbat is no longer a part of the tradition of most Christians. The few who do observe it often "change" Shabbat to Sunday. The assumption is that Shabbat is no longer valid since it is not clearly commanded in the New Testament.

There is a major problem with this point of view. Where does God say that only commandments in the New Testament are valid? To decide that three-fourths of the Bible contains no commandments for today is dangerous and offensive to God, who revealed himself through the whole of Scripture. Furthermore, Isaiah mentions Shabbat in a New Testament context:

> And the foreigners who join themselves to ADONAI to serve him, to love the name of ADONAI, and to be his workers, all who keep my Shabbat and do not profane it, and hold fast to my covenant, I will bring them to my holy mountain and make them joyful in my house of prayer; their burnt offerings and sacrifices will be accepted on my altar; for my house will be called a house of prayer for all peoples. (Isa. 56:6–7)

As nearly any commentary will tell you, this passage is a promise that is still future, for the time of Messiah's kingdom. We are told that Gentiles will keep Shabbat during the future kingdom of Messiah. Can there be any justification then for ignoring the fourth commandment today?

Working on Shabbat doesn't seem wrong to people who are not accustomed to keeping the commandment. That is the real problem. Most people assume that right and wrong should be obvious. It is obviously wrong to steal. If the Bible did not tell us that stealing is wrong we would still know it. But working on Shabbat is not obviously wrong. We only know it is wrong because God tells us so.

What Are We Commanded to Do on Shabbat?

First, it is important to address a myth. The myth is that God requires us to hold a corporate worship service on Shabbat. That is a Jewish custom, not a biblical commandment. The Scripture sometimes cited as commanding worship on Shabbat is as follows: "But the seventh day is a Shabbat of complete rest, a holy convocation" (Lev. 23:3). In some other translations "holy convocation" is "sacred assembly." Some feel that this is a commandment to gather in assembly (convocation) on Shabbat.

Shabbat is not about holding a worship service, as we saw in the chapter "The *Torah* and the believer," although it is good to worship God any day of the week. Christians have a tradition of worshipping on Sunday because it is the day many say Yeshua rose from the dead. This tradition is fine as long as someone doesn't make it a rule. Messianic Jewish congregations follow instead the Jewish tradition of worshipping on Shabbat, the seventh day. This tradition was necessary in the ancient world, where Shabbat was the only day that work could be laid aside. The truth is, you can worship God on Tuesday if you like, but if you want to obey God and be blessed in the way he wants you to be blessed, rest on Shabbat.

The commandment is simple:

Remember the day, Shabbat, to set it apart for God. You have six days to labor and do all your work, but the seventh day is a Shabbat for *ADONAI* your God. On it, you are not to do any kind of work—not you, your son or your daughter, your male or your female slave, not your livestock, and not the foreigner staying with you inside the gates of your property. For in six days *Adonai* made heaven and earth, the sea and everything in them; but on the seventh day he rested. This is why *Adonai* blessed the day, Shabbat, and separated it for himself. (Exod. 20:8–11)

No work should be done on Shabbat. In practice, it has never been easy to define exactly what "work" means. If you ever studied physics, you know that any motion at all is "work." The Bible gives some clues to God's definition of work in a few passages.

A fire is not to be kindled on Shabbat (Exod. 35:3). This commandment must be understood in the context of life in Moses' day. The fire was the source of cooking and heat in the home. Fire was necessary to life. The commandment was not, "You shall not have fire," but "you shall not kindle fire." In other words, the fire was to be kindled and kept alive from the day before Shabbat. The principle is this: Any work that can reasonably be prepared before Shabbat should not be done on Shabbat.

A similar clue is found in Numbers 15:32. A man was caught gathering sticks on Shabbat and was executed for his crime. The issue here was doing necessary work, for sticks were needed, but he was doing it at the wrong time.

One other clue is found in Nehemiah 10:31. The people were buying and selling on Shabbat. Nehemiah prohibited this. They were buying and selling from Gentiles who did not keep Shabbat. The principles seems to be that we should not make others work on Shabbat by buying or selling.

The rabbis add many laws to the Shabbat commandment by prohibiting 39 categories of work. Their definitions and prohibitions seem to go far beyond the simple teaching of Scripture. For example, walking to synagogue, which is harder work than driving, is commanded because the Bible says to rest your animals on Shabbat. The car is compared to a horse and the rabbis say that we must rest out cars. This is going too far, in my opinion, and adding unnecessary rules to a beautiful day of rest.

What about little things like clearing the table after meals and preparing food? It is best to do as much cooking as possible the day before Shabbat so that there will be plenty of time for rest. But it is not wrong to do the minimum work necessary to live and operate. Clearing the table is necessary for carrying on a household and is not wrong. The issue is to plan ahead and prevent as much work as possible. Thus, Friday morning and afternoon are times for preparation in a Jewish home. The house is thoroughly cleaned and food is prepared for Friday night and Saturday ahead of time. Yardwork is either done ahead or saved for Saturday after sundown or Sunday. That little bit of extra work pays off on Friday night and Saturday as life slows down and everyone rests in Yeshua, the Lord of Shabbat.

Does the New Testament Abolish the Shabbat Commandment?

One particular verse in the New Testament is often used to suggest that God no longer commands us to rest on Shabbat:

> One person considers some days more holy than others, while someone else regards them as all being alike. What is important is for each to be fully convinced in his own mind. (Rom. 14:5)

In interpreting this passage it is important to remember that the primary audience of Paul's letter to Rome was Gentiles. These Gentiles in Rome had an anti-Jewish prejudice. Therefore, Paul is not talking really about Shabbat or Jewish holidays here, but days and ceremonies common to the Gentiles.

The problem Paul is addressing is the radical change that faith in Yeshua brought to the lifestyle of these Gentiles. Many of the ceremonies and customs they had celebrated their whole life were now questionable activities. Many decisions had to be made about keeping various feasts and ceremonies. Paul's point is that there is room for different approaches and no one should look down on those who made different lifestyle decisions. Paul is not saying that one of God's commandments is no longer valid. If he were, you can bet that he would be much more clear about it.

The Traditional Shabbat Meal

On Friday night, just before sundown, it is traditional to hold a special meal with a little ceremony. This is not a part of the biblical commandment, but is a beautiful part of Jewish tradition. The blessings that are said over the bread and wine (or juice) on Friday

141

night were used by Yeshua (see Matt. 26:26–27) at the Passover. The basic order of the Friday night meal is simple and a wonderful family ceremony. Especially if you have children, ceremonies like this add to the life of a family as children look forward every week to the blessings that bring family together.

The start of the Friday night meal is a table spread with a tablecloth and arrayed with two loaves of *challah* bread, two candles, and a glass of wine or grape juice (usually in a silver cup called a *kiddush* cup). As the family gathers around the table, the woman of the house covers her head with a scarf, lights the candles, covers her eyes with her hands, and recites a prayer over the candles:

> *Barukh atah ADONAI, Eloheinu melekh ha'olam, asher kidshanu b'Yeshua haMashiach Or-Ha'Olam. Amen.*

> Blessed are you, O Lord our God, King of the Universe, who has sanctified us in Yeshua the Messiah, the Light of the World. Amen.

The traditional Hebrew prayer is a little different, saying that we are sanctified and commanded to light the candles. Some Jewish believers do not use the traditional prayer because we are not commanded to light the candles.

Following the woman's prayer, it is customary for the man to lift up the *kiddush* cup of juice or wine and recite:

> *Barukh atah ADONAI, Eloheinu melekh ha'olam, borey pri hagafen. Amen.*

> Blessed are you, O Lord our God, King of the Universe, who created the fruit of the vine. Amen.

The man may drink the cup or pass it around for everyone to drink. He then tears off a piece of the challah bread and recites:

> *Barukh atah ADONAI, Eloheinu melekh ha'olam, ha-motzi lechem min ha'aretz. Amen.*

Blessed are you, O Lord our God, King of the Universe, who brings forth bread from the earth. Amen.

He then passes the bread around and everyone eats a piece. Some people then continue with blessings over the children. The boys are called up and the father holds his hand on their head:

Yesimkha Elohim k'Ephraim v'kheeM'nasheh.

May God make you like Ephraim and Manasseh.

Then the girls are called up, hands placed on their heads and:

Yismekh Elohim k'Sarah, Rivka, Rakhel, v'Leah.

May God make you like Sarah, Rebecca, Rachel, and Leah.

After the blessings are recited, the man sometimes will read from Proverbs 31:10–31 in honor of his wife. Then the family will enjoy the meal. After the meal it is traditional to sing praise songs together.

On Saturday night, following dinner, there is a traditional closing service for Shabbat called the Havdalah service, which can be found in any *siddur*. By bringing in Shabbat with a ceremonial meal and closing it out with one, you will draw attention to the blessedness of the day. You might add your own family traditions to the day to make it even more special. If you hold Shabbat with an attitude of joy, it will be the day of the week that everyone looks forward to the most.

(For more information, I recommend *The Sabbath: Entering God's Rest*, by Barry and Steffi Rubin; see bibliography.)

143

Holidays

The New Testament is replete with references to the Levitical holidays and to one additional holiday, Hanukkah (the Feast of Dedication). The Last Supper, of course, was a Passover. Paul also refers to Yeshua as "our Pesach [Passover] lamb" (1 Cor. 5:7). Yeshua used the Feast of Booths (Tabernacles or *Sukkot*) and the Feast of Dedication (Hanukkah) as occasions to speak at the Temple (John 7:2; 10:22). God chose to initiate his congregation, to reveal to the world his choosing to place his favor upon the followers of Yeshua, on *Shavu'ot* (Pentecost) (Acts 2:1–13). Paul also was eager to get to Jerusalem to celebrate *Shavu'ot* and in another year didn't want to leave Ephesus until after he had celebrated *Shavu'ot* (Acts 20:16; 1 Cor. 16:8).

If the Jewish, or biblical, holidays were such an important part of the practice of the early followers of Yeshua, you might wonder why they are no longer practiced in most churches. The answer, in brief, is that the leaders who succeeded the apostles (emissaries) for the first few centuries of church history were by and large anti-Semitic. A study of church history will reveal that these leaders were brought up in Roman anti-Semitism, made disparaging remarks about Jewish people, and removed Jewish customs from the practice of the congregations. A simple overview of this tragic history can be found in Michael Brown's *Our Hands Are Stained With Blood* or Stan Telchin's *Abandoned* (see bibliography).

The truth is that the non-Jewish church would have done far better to practice the Jewish holidays. The culture of Yeshua and the apostles is rich, as anyone worshipping in a Messianic congregation can testify. Many non-Jewish believers are celebrating the holidays now and teaching them to their children. How much more should Jewish believers be enriched and nourished by these special celebrations of God's work in history.

The Basics of the Jewish Holidays

There are seven holidays prescribed in Leviticus 23: Passover, Unleavened Bread, Firstfruits, *Shavu'ot*, Trumpets (called Rosh HaShanah today), Yom Kippur, and *Sukkot* (Tabernacles). Added to these seven are one from the book of Esther, *Purim*, and one from the time between the Hebrew Bible and the New Testament, Hanukkah. These nine holidays are celebrations of what God has done in history. Following is a description of the holidays in the order of the secular calendar, relevant Scripture passages, and a brief description of the celebration of the holidays. For a fuller understanding, I recommend *God's Appointed Times* by Barney Kasdan.

1. *Purim*, the Feast of Lots—This joyous celebration occurs in late February or in March, before the Passover. On the Jewish calendar, *Purim* begins on the 14th of Adar. The origin of *Purim* is found in the book of Esther. *Purim* gets its name from the lots that Haman cast to decide on which day to destroy the Jews. The modern celebration includes telling the story of Esther, with cheering for Mordechai and booing for Haman. Special cookies, called *hamantashen*, are made and gift baskets of fruit are traditionally taken to those in need.

2. *Passover*—This is the first night of the week of Unleavened Bread during late March or April. The story of the first Passover can be found in Exodus 12–14. On the Jewish calendar, the Passover Seder begins on the 15th of Nisan, when the family gathers for a Seder or Passover Feast. Extended family or even friends are often invited over for the Passover Seder. The order of service for the Passover Seder is found in a book called a Haggadah. If you have celebrated Passover all your life before coming to know Yeshua, you have yet to experience the joy of a Messianic Seder, which is the origin of the Communion or Lord's Supper service in some congregations. Yeshua is the Passover lamb and the whole Seder points to him, even specific customs practiced by the Jewish community.

3. *Unleavened Bread*—This is the rest of the week of Passover. The primary reminder of God during these seven days is the absence of leaven. This is a time to commemorate the Exodus of the Jewish people from Egypt. Eating *matzah* (unleavened bread) for seven days will help you to identify with those who came out of Egypt and went into the wilderness.

4. *Firstfruits*—This Jewish holiday is not emphasized by modern Judaism, primarily because its provisions had to do with a ceremony in the Temple. In Leviticus 23:9–14, this ceremony is

described. The priest was to wave before the Lord a bundle from the first standing grain of the barley crop. Significantly, Yeshua rose on the day of Firstfruits, a fact which Paul refers to in 1 Corinthians 15:20 and 23. Thus, Messianic Jewish believers can celebrate the Resurrection of Yeshua, not with pagan symbols like eggs, but by blessing a loaf of bread (barley if you can get it) or a cup of grain and remembering the story of the Resurrection of the Messiah.

5. *Shavu'ot* —Also know as Pentecost or the Feast of Weeks, this celebration is described in Leviticus 23:15–21. It usually occurs somewhere around May, or the 6th of Sivan on the Jewish calendar. *Shavu'ot* is a celebration of the wheat harvest. Thus, it is traditional to set the table with greenery for a *Shavu'ot* meal as a harvest celebration and to read the story of Ruth, which involves the wheat harvest. Another Jewish tradition is to eat dairy products, reminding us of the life-giving milk of the Bible, and to stay up late the night after *Shavu'ot* studying the Bible. As followers of Yeshua, this is a good time to read the story of a special *Shavu'ot* in Acts 2.

6. *Trumpets*—Also known as *Yom Teru'ah* (Day of Trumpets) or *Rosh HaShanah*, as it is called by modern Judaism. Today this holiday is the Jewish New Year and is a time for sending cards. But according to the Bible, it is a day for blowing the ram's horn, or shofar. Rosh HaShanah starts out the High Holidays of the fall of the year and occurs in September or October. The holiday is described in Leviticus 23:23–25 and falls on the 1st of Tishri on the Jewish calendar. A special service is held in synagogues, as well as in most Messianic congregations, for the blowing of the shofar. The shofar is most likely blown as a call to repentance in preparation for Yom Kippur, which comes only nine days later. Rosh HaShanah may also serve for believers as a time to look forward to the return of Yeshua, who will be preceded by a great blast of the trumpet (1 Thess. 4:16).

7. *Yom Kippur*—Also known as the Day of Atonement, this is the day that God would have the high priest come into the Most Holy Place with blood to atone for the sin of the whole nation (Lev. 16). Coming only nine days after Rosh HaShanah, Yom Kippur falls on the 10th of Tishri on the Jewish calendar. For many Jewish people this day is a day of fasting and repentance, hoping that God will accept repentance and give another year

of life and blessing. Followers of Yeshua could look at the holiday in more than one way. We could celebrate the final atonement made by Yeshua on the tree. Or we could join the rest of the Jewish community in fasting and confessing our sins to God. Even though we have forgiveness already in Yeshua, we must confess our sins before God to maintain intimacy with him.

8. *Sukkot*—Known in English as the Feast of Tabernacles or Feast of Booths, this is a joyous harvest celebration. Families build a booth, similar to a brush arbor, and decorate it with branches and fruit. This booth, or *sukkah*, is a place to hold prayers in, to eat meals, and (if the climate allows) to live in for the seven days of *Sukkot*. God commanded Israel to live in booths for seven days in Leviticus 23:33–43 as a memorial of the wilderness period, when Israelites lived in tents for 40 years. *Sukkot* is about dwelling with God and looks forward to the Messianic kingdom where God will dwell (Tabernacle) among us. One fascinating Scripture says that even Gentile nations will come to Jerusalem for *Sukkot* in the kingdom of Messiah (Zech. 14:16–19). A great way to celebrate *Sukkot* today is to build a *sukkah* in your yard and invite friends to learn about *Sukkot* and pray and eat in the *sukkah*.

9. *Hanukkah*—Also known as the Feast of Dedication, this eight-day holiday is not commanded in the Bible. The origin of Hanukkah lies in the time between the Hebrew Bible and the New Testament. Like *Purim*, Hanukkah celebrates a time when Israel was delivered from enemies. Yeshua used Hanukkah as an occasion to teach about his Messiahship and his deity in John 10:22–39. A nine-branched menorah (lampstand) is lit (one candle added each night) through the eight days of Hanukkah. The story of the Maccabees and the origin of Hanukkah is told. Believers in Yeshua might add to the holiday by reading Scriptures which speak of God and of Yeshua being like light.

What About Yeshua's Birth and Resurrection?

Since God chose to use holidays to commemorate his great acts in the history of Israel, it makes sense that the incarnation of Yeshua, which is a term for his deity joining with a human nature at his birth, and the resurrection should be celebrated. Why celebrate the Exodus from Egypt and omit God becoming a man and rising from the dead?

Part of the controversy about Christmas and Easter, the traditional Christian celebrations of these events, has to do with pagan customs added to the holiday. Eggs and bunnies, as well as the name Easter, arise from a time when the celebration of the resurrection was joined to a feast for a pagan fertility goddess named Ishtar (Ashtoreth in the Hebrew Bible). The date of Christmas, December 25, was chosen because of a pagan celebration of the winter solstice called Saturnalia.

Some people feel all right about keeping customs with pagan roots, as long as they are no longer thought of as pagan. For example, most Christians today would see eggs at Easter as a symbol of resurrection (rather than their original meaning as fertility symbols). Others feel that we should separate ourselves from any custom with a pagan origin. Some desire to celebrate the incarnation and resurrection on different dates than the traditional church does.

The incarnation and resurrection ought to be celebrated. God delights in holidays that commemorate his great acts. Issues of how and when to celebrate these events should be prayerfully thought out. Below is one possible approach, but not by any means the only one.

Call Resurrection Day either by that name or by the Jewish holiday on which it fell, Firstfruits. Avoid eggs and bunnies as a part of the holiday. Celebrate it either on the day of Firstfruits or on the Sunday following Passover. Teach the resurrection story to your family. The tradition of eating sweets on Resurrection Day can be a beautiful one if you use it to point to the sweetness of the promise of resurrection.

There is no problem with the name Christmas, since Christ means Messiah. Some people call it Messiahmas. Although choosing a date to celebrate this holiday can be problematic, keeping it on December 25 will not really be following a pagan custom as long as we avoid traditions involving Yule, the pagan holiday, and Saturnalia. Whatever day you celebrate it, telling the story of Yeshua's birth should be the center of the holiday, and not Santa

Claus or gifts. Gifts can add to the holiday if we point them to God's gift of sending his Son to be our Messiah.

The Purpose of the Holidays

The biblical and spiritual holidays serve several important functions. They are an opportunity for education, teaching our families and congregations about the history of Israel and of God's work in history. They help us to be closer to God by living out that history in the yearly rhythm of life. They help us never to forget the things that are most important and help us look ahead to the Messianic kingdom. For a follower of Yeshua, holidays are more than celebration and remembrance; they are worship.

Tzitzit and Tallit (Fringes and Prayer Shawl)

One of God's more unusual commandments to Israel was that fringes were to be worn on the corner of garments:

> Speak to the people of Israel, instructing them to make, through all their generations, *tzitziyot* on the corners of their garments, and to put with the *tzitzit* on each corner a blue thread. It is to be a *tzitzit* for you to look at and thereby remember all of ADONAI's *mitzvot* [commandments] and obey them, so that you won't go around wherever your own heart and eyes lead you to prostitute yourselves; but it will help you to remember and obey all my *mitzvot* and be holy for your God. (Num. 15:38–40)

The word *tzitziyot* (plural for *tzitzit*) refers to a lock of hair or fringe of thread. In Ezekiel 8:3, we read of God grabbing hold of the prophet by a lock of his hair (*tzitzit rosh*). In ancient times, these fringes were a part of one's actual outer garment. At different times the styles of outer garments changed, but most were in the general fashion of a robe. These ancient garments easily accommodated fringes at the corners.

Now that men no longer dress in robes, the style of *tzitzit* has changed. In modern Judaism, only the men wear *tzitzit*. Women are said by the rabbis to be exempt from certain commandments. Orthodox men wear an undershirt with *tzitzit* on it, called the *tallit katan*, and the fringes are left hanging out from under the outer shirt. During Saturday morning service and at other daytime services, a special outer garment called the *tallit* (*tallis* amongst Ashkenazi Jews) or Prayer Shawl is worn. This garment also has *tzitzit* on it. Less religious people do not wear the undershirt during the week, but only the prayer shawl during worship services.

The Purpose of the Commandment

According to the passage in Numbers 15, the *tzitziyot* would help Israelites to avoid sin. It would mark them as people of Israel, the holy people of the covenant. Wearing a special marker on the garment would remind them of the commandments and of their special place in the world as God's covenant people and as priests to the nations.

The text in Numbers says that the *tzitziyot* would keep Israelites from going "around wherever your own heart and eyes lead you." In other words, wearing the markers of a holy people would keep Israelites from blending into a Gentile crowd and entering pagan worship, places of sorcery and divination, or places of sexual immorality.

The Relevance of the Commandment Today

There is room to disagree about the use of *tzitziyot* today. Some will see commandment to wear the fringes seen as still binding, since it is to be throughout the generations. If this position is taken, then it seems that both men and women should wear them. The argument from the rabbis that women are exempt is not based upon scriptural considerations, but issues of Jewish rabbinical law. Some would argue for wearing them all the time and others on a prayer shawl only in religious services. However, the original commandment suggests that they should be worn at all times.

For those who decide to wear the fringes, there is a consideration of style. The current Jewish styles of the *tallit katan* and the regular *tallit* are not set in stone. God merely said to put fringes on the corners of the garments, with no specification as to the general look of these tassels or fringes. Creative individuals could certainly design styles that are fashionable, with a great deal of freedom for innovation.

The other possibility is that the *tzitzit* commandment is a part of a whole set of commandments that have been abolished in Yeshua. Ephesians 2:14–15 tells us that Yeshua has broken down the dividing wall between Jewish and Gentile followers of God. He has destroyed the separation sanctioned in *Torah* between Jewish and Gentile people. Since the command to wear *tzitziyot* marks Jewish people as separate from Gentiles, it could be seen as one of the mitzvot that is done away with by Yeshua. If this is true, then we may still derive a great principle from the commandment. Reminders of God's commandments, whether they be a part of a special garment or some other object that reminds us of God, can be useful to us in keeping the commandments of God.

Praying the *Siddur*

To some people the idea of praying pre-written prayers is foreign, or at least unusual. Many are accustomed to extemporaneous prayers only, offering to God spontaneous words of praise and petition. Certainly the Bible indicates that spontaneous prayer is a part of our communication with him. The patriarchs, prophets, and apostles spoke to God freely in this way. But the Bible also models for us the use of pre-written prayers.

The Psalms are the prayers and hymns of Israel. Often it is obvious that the words of the psalms were composed as a spontaneous prayer by David or some other who faced difficult problems. Yet the written prayers of David and the other psalmists became the prayers and worship songs of the Israelites. The Lord's Prayer is another example of a model prayer handed down to us for our use.

Modern Judaism emphasizes the use of pre-written prayers almost to the exclusion of spontaneous prayer. This extreme emphasis has its spiritual problems. Those who believe they can only speak to God words written by others long ago will not have the kind of intimacy with God that he desires. But as a part of a balanced prayer life, model prayers have great value. By praying words written by David in the Psalms, other biblical prayers, prayers written by believers who lived before us, or the traditional Jewish prayers found in the *siddur*, we express to God great thoughts that are beyond what we ourselves would have been able to say. There is greater selflessness in praying the words of other people and this can be an advantage in making prayer something greater than ourselves.

What is the *Siddur*?

The *siddur* is a collection of Jewish prayers for use daily, on Shabbat, and during the synagogue service. There are different editions, the most notable differences being between the Ashkenazi and Sephardic *siddurs*. Yet the basics of the prayers are the same in various *siddurs*, since many of the prayers go back to a time before Yeshua was born.

Prayers in the *siddur* cover a wide variety of topics. Life after death, the restoration of Israel, the rebuilding of the Temple, the coming of the Messiah, and similar topics are emphasized in parts of the prayers. Repentance for sin and praise to the Holy One are the most common themes.

The Orthodox Pattern: *Shacharit, Minchah,* and *Ma'ariv*

Based upon the example of Daniel, who prayed three times a day (Dan. 6:10), the rabbis have devised three daily prayer times. The *shacharit*, or morning prayer, is the most involved. In addition to reciting prayers from the *siddur*, this is the time when the *tzitzit* are put on for the day and the tefillin are wrapped on for the duration of the prayer time (see *God's Appointed Customs* by Barney Kasdan to learn how to don the tefillin). The *minchah*, or afternoon service, and the *ma'ariv*, or evening service, use basically the same prayers, but without the tefillin. Following the Orthodox prayer schedule requires a great deal of time.

Should believers follow this schedule? Certainly one might choose to do so. Neither the prayers nor the schedule are a biblical commandment. Those who choose to follow this pattern will benefit from intimate familiarity with the many Scriptures that are a part of the prayers. Yet, the spiritual gain from this rigorous exercise is small in comparison with the time and effort spent. The rabbinical rationale for the rigorous prayer is duty. They believe that this is a commandment.

Furthermore, they also believe that following this prayer schedule is a part of their redemption. The Orthodox community long ago decided that prayer, repentance, and good deeds replace the sacrifices. In fact, the daily prayer times are even related by the rabbis to the morning and afternoon sacrifice at the Temple. The evening prayer is related to the burning of any leftover meat on the altar at night in the Temple. In other words, the Orthodox have a very different motivation from us in using this rigorous prayer schedule.

Suggestions For Use of the *Siddur*

Some of the prayers from the *siddur* existed before the time of Yeshua. In fact, it is clear from the New Testament that he knew of these prayers and used them. Yeshua used the Jewish blessings

over bread and wine (Luke 9:16; 22:19, 20; 24:30). His model
prayer, often called the Lord's Prayer, bears a resemblance to certain lines from the Jewish prayers known as the *Kaddish* and
Amidah:

> May his great name be exalted and sanctified in the world
> that he created as he willed. May he give reign to his king-
> ship in your lifetimes and in your days, and in the lifetimes
> of the entire family of Israel, swiftly and soon.
> (*Kaddish*, opening lines)

> We shall sanctify your name in this world, just as they sanc-
> tify it in heaven above. (*Amidah*, third benediction)

Such ancient words and traditions can have a beautiful significance
for us.

One caution is necessary in using the *siddur*. Not often, but
occasionally, some of the concepts in the *siddur* are opposed to
faith in Yeshua. For example, in the morning blessings, there is a
line that reads, "for none like Moses arose again." This was true
up until the time that Yeshua came, but Yeshua was one greater
than Moses. Moses was God's messenger. Yeshua is God. Therefore, the Messianic Jew using the *siddur* will need to modify any
such line, "none arose like Moses until Yeshua." Another example
of this problem is the use of the term "commanded" in some of
the blessings. In the blessing over the lighting of the candles,
there is a phrase "commanded us to light the candles of Shabbat."
We have not been commanded to light candles. The rabbis command it, but we do not serve them, but God. Modifications will
be necessary on rare occasions when praying from the *siddur*.

Having said that, it is also important to point out that the
siddur is not filled with unscriptural ideas. The opposite is true.
Many of the lines of the *siddur* are a direct quotation of Scripture.
You certainly do not have to worry that praying the *siddur* will in-
doctrinate you to Orthodox Judaism. Its prayers are almost completely consistent with the whole of God's truth, including the
New Testament.

There are a number of ways that you can use the *siddur*, even
if you do not follow the Orthodox pattern. First of all, there are

blessings customarily recited over ordinary events that show us God's hand in our lives. For example, when you hear thunder, you can recite the blessing, "Blessed are you, Lord our God, King of the Universe, for your strength and power fill the universe." Upon seeing a beautiful scene in nature, you can recite, "Blessed are you, Lord our God, King of the Universe, who has made such in your universe." These blessings, listed as the *Berakhot* or Blessings of Praise and Gratitude in the *siddur* make a way to see God in the things we encounter in daily life and to remember him at all times.

Another way to use the *siddur* is to periodically set aside some time and pray through parts of it. The rabbis insist that praying in Hebrew is better. There is no justification for this claim. Feel free to pray in Hebrew or whatever language you are accustomed to speaking. You might decide to go through the whole *shacharit* one day or simply to pray the *Amidah*, the *Kaddish*, or some other prayer from the *siddur*.

You certainly can live and serve Yeshua without a *siddur*. But why not enjoy and learn about this part of the rich heritage of the Jewish people? A Messianic Jewish *siddur* is available (*Siddur For Messianic Jews* by Dr. John Fischer and Dr. David Bronstein; see bibliography) and recommended. Otherwise, Artscroll produces a very useful *siddur* in Hebrew and English. This *siddur* by Artscroll is available in Jewish bookstores and catalogues and comes in Ashkenazi and Sephardic versions. Used as a tool in prayer, the *siddur* will add richness and beauty to your communication with God.

Kosher

Ask different people the meaning of kosher and you'll get various answers. To some it means following a very rigorous set of laws. There are multiple sets of dishes—one for meat, another for milk, and a third for Passover. There are special precautions taken, such as having pots and pans blowtorched at Passover to remove even the slightest trace of leaven. There are special places to buy kosher meat, which must be butchered under rabbinic supervision and by a *shochet* (ritual butcher) who insures that no nicks are in the blade of the slaughtering knife. One nick in the blade renders the entire animal unusable because the rabbis say this would render the carcass torn meat, forbidden by *Torah*. The rules for this type of kosher are so numerous and confusing, that the only way to keep it is to buy all of your food from a kosher store.

For others it just means avoiding certain meats and keeping meat and milk separate. For still others it just means avoiding the meats that the Bible prohibits Jewish people from eating. For some Messianic Jews, kosher has been a way of life even prior to knowing Yeshua. For most Messianic Jews, however, kosher is a relatively foreign concept.

The Biblical Issue

In Leviticus 11, God tells the Israelites what meats they may eat and what meats they may not eat. No reason is given for the meats allowed and the meats forbidden. Some have suggested that the issue is health. The most famous of all forbidden meats is pork, which is known to be a meat high in fat and cholesterol. Yet, not all of the forbidden meats are unhealthy and not all of the permitted meats are low-fat options. Is the meat of a catfish (not kosher) really less healthy than beef (kosher)?

Others have suggested that the forbidden meats had symbolic value that is difficult for us to understand today. Thousands of years have passed since the days these laws were given. We are not used to the kind of thinking that existed when the world was primarily populated by people who worshipped numerous gods and spirits. Animals were classified by certain traits and habits, such as hoofs and method of eating. Animals that mixed various traits, such as those that had split hoofs like cattle but did not chew the cud, were forbidden in God's law. Perhaps such animals were thought by the pagans to have magical significance and God wanted his people to avoid them.

We may never know why God forbade certain meats. But we do not have to know. We can obey the commandments without fully understanding them. The following are God's criteria for permissible meats and non-permissible meats:

> Land animals that have split hooves and chew the cud are kosher.
> Land animals that do not meet both qualifications are not kosher.
> Water animals with fins and scales are kosher.
> Water animals that do not have both are not kosher.
> Birds of prey and carrion are not kosher, whereas fowl (chickens and ducks) are kosher.
> All insect other than grasshoppers are not kosher, but grasshoppers are.

Thus, for example, pig meat and horse meat are not kosher since they do not meet both qualifications. Catfish, having no scales, is not kosher, and neither are any of the shellfish, nor lobster and shrimp. The most commonly eaten meats in Western society forbidden by the kosher laws are pork, lobster, and shrimp.

Eating these forbidden meats is said to make the worshipper "unclean." Being unclean prohibits a worshipper from entering a sacred area or eating a sacred offering. Does this distinction between clean and unclean have any relevance to our day?

Is Kosher Necessary Today?

This is a vexing question. On the one hand, the issue of clean and unclean has no relevance today. The laws of clean and unclean had to do with sacred areas in the Tabernacle (and later the Temple) and with sacred objects (the meat of offerings). Clean and unclean was not an issue of sin. Sometimes an act of love could cause one to be unclean. Touching a corpse or touching one's wife during her menstruation would make one unclean. Sometimes it would be necessary to touch a corpse, but the uncleanness was still passed on even though the contact was not sinful.

157

What did it mean to be unclean? Could the worshipper not pray, sing praises to God, or recite the Scriptures? Certainly uncleanness did not prevent prayer or any other relationship with God. Uncleanness merely prevented contact with sacred areas and objects. Sacred areas and objects do not exist today. Therefore, uncleanness has no effect on someone today.

This could be a good argument to say that kosher laws are irrelevant today. However, God doesn't just say that eating unkosher food makes one unclean, he expressly forbids it, "do not make yourselves unclean with them, do not defile yourselves with them" (Lev. 11:43). Thus, it could be argued that the kosher laws are not only an issue of clean and unclean, but also a commandment.

What About Milk and Meat?

The rabbis forbid any intermixture of milk and meat on the basis of Exodus 23:19, "You are not to boil a young animal in its mother's milk." The origin of this prohibition is somewhat of a mystery. A manuscript found at Ugarit, a place peopled by the very Canaanites whom Israel drove out of the land, shows that boiling animals in milk was a magical ritual (*The Bible Student's Commentary: Exodus* by W. H. Gispen, p. 232; see bibliography). Milk was believed to have magical value as the seed of life. Boiling an animal in milk gave the flesh life-giving power in pagan thought (Gispen, p. 232). Thus, God was forbidding Israelites to practice this pagan custom.

Yet, the rabbis take this commandment to an extreme. They want to avoid any possibility of milk and meat, even the smallest molecule of each, ever mixing, lest one anger God by accidentally boiling a small particle of meat in milk. They even forbid using the same dishes for meat and milk products, necessitating two sets of dishes. Nor can meat and milk be eaten at the same meal (no cheeseburgers).

Interestingly, when three angelic beings came to visit Abraham in Genesis 18, he served them a meal which the rabbis would forbid:

> Then he took curds, milk, and the calf which he had prepared, and set it all before the men; and he stood by them under the trees as they ate. (18:8)

Clearly there is nothing wrong with eating milk and meat together if these angelic visitors from God ate them with Abraham. But even without this scriptural example we would be able to see the error in the rabbinical ruling. God's original commandment had nothing to do with separate dishes, but simply forbids boiling a young animal in its own mother's milk.

What About Kosher Meat and Blood?

Because God uses blood to make atonement, he forbids the Israelites to eat it (Lev. 17:10–12). This commandment is also for Gentiles (Lev. 17:10,12) and was given to Noah before there even were Jewish people (Gen. 9:4). We are not to eat meat with the blood left deliberately in it, nor are we to drink blood.

The rabbis have special laws intended to maximize the drainage of blood from meat when it is slaughtered. This includes soaking the meat in saltwater to remove even more blood than can be drained during slaughtering. Is it necessary then for us to buy kosher meat?

The truth is that non-kosher slaughtering also drains the blood from meat. God forbids eating meat in which the blood is deliberately left in, but not from eating normally slaughtered, blood-drained meat. The meat sold in grocery stores is drained of blood. Forbidden meat would be from an animal strangled so as to hold maximum blood (Acts 15:29).

What About Kosher and Gentiles?

The only prohibition for Gentiles is the eating of blood. Dead carcasses were prohibited to Jews but were allowed to be sold to Gentiles (Deut. 14:21). There is no reason why a Gentile should be forbidden to eat pork or other non-kosher meats.

Doesn't the New Testament Change the Kosher Laws?

In Mark 7:19, some modern translations read, "Thus he declared all foods clean" (NASB). Some take this to be Yeshua abolishing the kosher laws. Yet Yeshua is not discussing kosher, but rather the Pharisees' rules of handwashing. They believed that anyone who did not perform the handwashing ceremony before eating was eating non-kosher food. Yeshua's comment was that food going into our mouths goes through the digestive tract and is eliminated from the body, but the words we speak from our mouths to hurt others or to tell lies, these are what make us unclean. In other words, rituals before eating are not important, but watching our words is important.

Others say that God changed the kosher laws when he gave Peter a vision in Acts 10. A sheet came down from heaven with non-kosher animals in it and God said, "Eat." So, was God telling Peter to eat pork? According to the text itself, no, because the vision was symbolic. The non-kosher meat was symbolic of Gentiles who needed to hear the gospel. Peter was being commanded not to withhold Yeshua's salvation from the Gentiles. The text has nothing to do with the kosher laws.

Summary

Arguments can be made for and against the need for kosher laws today in the lives of Jewish believers. Clearly Gentiles may eat of any meat as long as they avoid eating blood. Even Jewish believers who do not believe that the kosher laws are still in effect may choose to avoid non-kosher meat out of custom or as a witness to the Jewish community. Each person will have to study the Scriptures and determine what God wants him to do. Since there is room for differing interpretations, it is important not to argue about this issue. If someone disagrees with you about the kosher laws, recognize that they may be right. If you abstain, do so freely out of love for God, and if you eat, do not be bothered by those who do not.

Headcoverings

The *kippah*, or *yarmulke*, is one of the most distinguishing features of a religious Jewish man. Religious Jewish women also cover their heads either with a wig (*sheitel*) or a scarf. Despite the practice of the Orthodox community today, headcoverings have not always been required by rabbinical law. In the Talmud, headcovering was optional (Nedarim 30b, cited in *God's Appointed Customs* by Barney Kasdan, p. 133).

Nor has rabbinical law required any one style of headcovering. At different times in history, Jewish men have worn a variety of styles to cover their heads. The particular headpiece worn by Jewish men today comes from Renaissance Italy, and was the fashion for that time. This is why the headcovering worn by the Pope, the head of the Catholic Church, is similar to the Jewish headcovering.

Nor is there agreement about when one's head must be covered. In modern Orthodox Judaism, the headcovering is to be worn all day long. Conservative and Reform Jewish men generally wear headcoverings only in the worship service.

The Jewish practice of covering the head dates back to the turban of the high priest (Exod. 28:4). The high priest was to wear a special headcovering when ministering in the Tabernacle. Because of this requirement, it was reasoned that covering the head is a sign of submission to God. Therefore, if the high priest was required to show this sign of submission, why not everyone? Some would argue that such a covering should be worn all the time, since God is always with us, or just when ministering before or worshipping God, since the high priest only wore it on such occasions.

Should Messianic Jews Wear Headcoverings?

The headcovering is a tradition, not a commandment. Therefore, this is a matter of choice. However, if you decide to wear a headcovering all day long, it would be vital that you also keep kosher and live in such a way as to avoid offending traditional Jews. Another option is to wear a headcovering only during worship services. If you do this, remember that you are doing it as a sign of submission to God, not as a rule. Because this is an issue of tradition, it is not appropriate to pressure others to follow your practice.

Doesn't the New Testament Forbid Headcoverings for Men?

Paul says in 1 Corinthians 11:4, "Every man who prays or prophesies wearing something down over his head brings shame to his head." Some have taken this verse to refer to the Jewish practice of covering the head, either with the *kippah* or with the prayer shawl. But several considerations make it apparent this is not what Paul is referring to.

First of all, the headcovering Paul speaks of is put down over (kata) the head. David Stern points out that this Greek word, kata, would not be appropriate to describe a hat, but refers to a veil (*Jewish New Testament Commentary*, p. 474). Likewise, Thayer agrees in his *Greek-English Lexicon of the New Testament*, translating the phrase as "a veil hanging down from his head" (p. 327). This headcovering is not a *yarmulke*, but a veil such as Gentile women wore in Corinth and in other parts of the ancient world. It was not thought fitting, in that culture, for a man to wear a veil. Women wore veils as a sign of modesty and, perhaps, to save the sight of the beauty of their hair for their husband only.

Second of all, Paul is primarily writing to Gentiles here anyway. Even if we could not determine that veils are the issue as opposed to hats, this is not a Jewish issue. Paul is not forbidding the use of a *kippah* or *yarmulke* in worship.

Is Paul commanding women, Jewish or Gentile, to cover their heads? This issue is hotly debated. Many take the position that Paul is talking here about a custom local to Corinth. He is addressing women, who are now free in Messiah, who are removing customs of propriety, such as headcovering, from their lifestyle. Paul is arguing that the authority of the husband is important and so these women should keep the custom of covering their heads. According to this position, Paul is expressing a principle of the authority of the husband but is not commanding all women in all cultures to cover their heads. Others point to the fact that Paul makes his argument from nature and from the existence of angels. This could be seen as evidence that this is a permanent principle.

The evidence seems to be in favor of the local custom view.

Paul says that a woman who refuses to wear a veil ought to shave her head. In other words, the issue is that the woman should not show her hair to other men besides her husband. This is a non-issue in most cultures. Yet even if women are not commanded in this passage to wear veils, modesty and a proper relationship with the husband are clearly commanded here.

Covering the Head With the Prayer Shawl

A custom amongst religious Jews is the covering of the head with the *tallit* during certain prayers. Generally covering the head is done during a particularly deep or moving prayer. This custom can be a fitting expression of devotion. If you worship in a Messianic congregation where the prayer shawl is used by some of the worshippers, then using the *tallit* to create a private prayer space between yourself and God may be helpful for you. It may lead you to be able to better focus on God. But following this custom to look more earnest in prayer and to give an appearance of devotion is inappropriate. Those who deliberately show off their devotion forfeit any reward from God (Matt. 6:5). If you cover your head, however you do it, with *kippah* or *tallit*, do it for God and God alone. If you leave your head uncovered, do it for the glory of God as well.

Conclusion

Shortly before the disciples saw Yeshua in his glory during his transfiguration (Matt. 17:1–8), he held an intimate talk with them. He explained what it means to walk as a disciple:

> Then Yeshua told his *talmidim* [disciples], "If anyone wants to come after me, let him say 'No' to himself, take up his execution-stake [cross], and keep following me. For whoever wants to save his own life will destroy it, but whoever destroys his life for my sake will find it. (Matt. 16:24–25)

The timing of Yeshua's lesson on discipleship was significant for the twelve apostles. Not only did it come shortly before the revelation of Yeshua's glory, it came right after he explained the suffering he would soon endure. As Matthew relates the story, "From this time on, Yeshua began making it clear to his talmidim that he had to go to Yerushalayim [Jerusalem] and endure much suffering . . ." (Matt. 16:21).

In between suffering and glory Yeshua explained discipleship. We are in between Yeshua's suffering and glory right now. Yes, he is already raised and sits at the right hand of the Father in glory. But that glory has yet to be revealed to the world as it will on that day when the Son of Man comes with the clouds of heaven.

So in between suffering and glory, we must walk as disciples. This may involve suffering and glory as well. The glories of life as Yeshua's disciple are many: peace about eternal life, intimacy with the God of Israel, the indwelling life of the Spirit of God in our inner being, and power to overcome sin and hurt. The suffering of the life of a disciple is really not so bad compared to the glory. As Paul said, "For our light and transient troubles are achieving for us an everlasting glory whose weight is beyond description. We concentrate not on what is seen but on what is not seen, since things seen are temporary, but things not seen are eternal" (2 Cor. 4:17–18).

Even so, living the Messianic Jewish life is not always easy. There may be division within your family. Living in obedience to God's commandments will sometimes be hard. Sharing your faith with friends is a risk that you may find stressful. Prayer is not always easy and faithfulness in prayer is resisted at every turn by the evil one. Even your reading of the scriptures will sometimes be hard. Some parts will confuse you or trouble you. Nothing will be more troubling than the realization that your life needs change. A day may come when our faith is illegal. Life in Yeshua involves some suffering.

This way of discipleship has been our subject in this book. We have explored together the basics of life in Yeshua, from the elementary principles of faith, to deeper issues of life in him, to potential problems we may face, to the Jewish elements of our lifestyle.

These principles are a guide and a beginning. But disciples never stop learning as long as they are disciples. Until you graduate into the kingdom, you are a disciple, a learner of the ways of Yeshua. Disciples can be called upon to change attitudes and even beliefs. We must always be open to change if God calls us to it through his scriptures, our friends in the congregation, or the circumstances God puts into our lives.

Whoever gives his life to Yeshua will gain back so much more in the end. Whoever tries to hold on to his own desires at Yeshua's expense is only hurting himself. As Yeshua said, "What good will it do if someone gains the whole world but forfeits his life?" (Matt. 16:26) Rather, forfeit your life for him and he will give a whole world, a better world than the one we live in now. That is the promise of discipleship—suffering and glory, the way of the walk with Yeshua.

Notes

1 Lew Wallace, *Ben-Hur*. New York: American Book-Stratford Press, p. 389.

2 Exodus Rabbah 2:5, cited in Joseph Telushkin, *Jewish Wisdom*. New York: William Morrow, 1994. pp. 285–286.

3 Yoma 35b, cited in Abraham Cohen, *Everyman's Talmud*. New York: Schocken, 1995. p. 136.

4 The Hebrew Bible (the Jewish Bible) is arranged in three sections: *Torah*, *Nevi'im* (Prophets), and *Ketuvim* (Writings). The organization of the Bible which is used in most Christian translations, and which is used here, is different.

5 Testimony of Yossi in David Zeidan, *Messiah Now*. Carlisle: OM Publishing, 1992. pp. 17–18.

6 C.S. Lewis, *Mere Christianity*. New York: MacMillan, 1960. p. 40.

7 Jim Cymbala, *Fresh Wind, Fresh Fire*. Grand Rapids: Zondervan, 1997. pp. 77–78.

8 Whereas the term *rabbi* literally means "my teacher," today it is a title given to someone who has received ordination from a rabbinic seminary. Thus, some feel uncomfortable with its use for those who have not been ordained.

9 Chuck Colson and Ellen Vaughn, *The Body*, pp. 339–340.

10 Kahan, Rabbi A. Y. *The Taryag Mitzvos*. Brooklyn: Keser Torah Publications, 1987.

Bibliography

Jewish Books

Brown, Michael. *Our Hands Are Stained With Blood*. Gaithersburg, Md.: Destiny Image Books, 1992.

Fischer, John and Bronstein, David. *Siddur For Messianic Jews*. Palm Harbor, Fla.: Menorah Ministries, 1988.

Kahan, Rabbi Aharan Yisroel. *The Taryag Mitzvos*. Brooklyn: Keser Torah Publications, 1987.

Kasdan, Barney. *God's Appointed Customs*. Baltimore, Md.: Lederer/Messianic Jewish Publishers, 1996.

Kasdan, Barney. *God's Appointed Times*. Baltimore, Md.: Lederer/ Messianic Jewish Publishers, 1993.

Rubin, Barry and Steffi. *The Sabbath: Entering God's Rest*. Baltimore, Md.: Lederer/Messianic Jewish Publishers, 1998.

Stern, David. *Complete Jewish Bible*. Clarksville, Md.: Jewish New Testament Publications, 1998.

Stern, David. *Jewish New Testament Commentary*. Clarksville, Md.: Jewish New Testament Publications, 1992.

Telchin, Stan. *Abandoned*. Grand Rapids: Baker Book House, 1997.

General Books

Bonhoeffer, Dietrich. *Psalms: The Prayerbook of the Bible*. Minneapolis: Augsburg Publishing, 1970.

Foster, Richard. *Prayer: Finding the Heart's True Home*. San Francisco: Harper Collins Publishers, 1992.

Hayford, Jack. *The Beauty of Spiritual Language*. Nashville: Thomas Nelson Publishers, 1996.

Johnstone, Patrick. *Operation World*. Grand Rapids: Zondervan, 1993.

Lawrence, Brother. *The Practice of the Presence of God*. Springdale, PA: Whitaker House Publishing, 1982.

Lewis, C.S. *Mere Christianity*. New York: MacMillan Publishing, 1943.

McQuilkin, Robertson. *The Great Omission*. Grand Rapids: Baker Book House, 1984.

Bible Study Library Resources

Bromiley, Geoffrey, ed. *The International Standard Bible Encyclopedia*. Grand Rapids: Eerdmans Publishing, 1979.

Douglas, J. D., ed. *The New Bible Dictionary*. Wheaton, Ill.: Tyndale House Publishers, 1982.

Fee, Gordon and Stuart, Douglas. *How To Read the Bible For All It's Worth*. Grand Rapids: Zondervan, 1982.

Gispen, W. H. *Exodus: Bible Student's Commentary*. Grand Rapids: Zondervan, 1982.

Morris, Leon, ed. *Tyndale New Testament Commentaries*. Grand Rapids: Eerdmans.

Nave, Orville J. *Nave's Topical Bible*. Nashville: The Southwestern Company, 1962.

Smith, Jerome H., ed. *The New Treasury of Scripture Knowledge*. Nashville: Thomas Nelson Publishers, 1992.

Strong, James. *The Exhaustive Concordance of the Bible*. McLean, Va.: MacDonald Publishing.

Wiseman, D. J., ed. *Tyndale Old Testament Commentaries*. Downers Grove, Ill.: InterVarsity Press.